SOUL-TO-SOUL CONNECTIONS

...simply the most beautifully written work I have read about the continuation of consciousness after physical transition... a "must read" for anyone who has lost a loved one and is struggling with the grieving process. Ms. Obley's descriptions of her contact with those who have passed through the veil of physicality validate the existence of the soul in the afterlife and offer hope to those who grieve the passing of life.
Rev. Barbara S. Delozier, Msc.D., host of the Metaphysical Edge radio

I cannot recommend this book strongly enough. Ms. Obley describes the emotions and concerns of both the living and those who have crossed over, cohesively presenting both viewpoints in an incredibly engaging manner. This book is a compelling read for those wondering about the everlasting journey of the soul.
Shay Parker, Founder of Best American Psychics

Through the years, I have worked with many healers and mediums; I would describe Carole Obley as both. Her whole mission in connecting with those here and beyond is to seek peace for them. She shares this wonderful gift with us page by page, and in the process, we just might find our own healing.
Carol Lee Espy, radio and TV producer/host

Very informative, inspiring and well written... A must read for anyone wanting to know about the experiences of life here and in the here-after...
Rev. John C.Lilek, Executive Director of the Universal Institute of Advanced Mediumship

Soul-to-Soul Connections

Comforting Messages from the Spirit World

Soul-to-Soul Connections

Comforting Messages from the Spirit World

Carole J. Obley

Winchester, UK
Washington, USA

First published by Sixth Books, 2013
Sixth Books is an imprint of John Hunt Publishing Ltd., Laurel House, Station Approach,
Alresford, Hants, SO24 9JH, UK
office1@jhpbooks.net
www.johnhuntpublishing.com
www.6th-books.com

For distributor details and how to order please visit the 'Ordering' section on our website.

Text copyright: Carole J. Obley 2011

ISBN: 978 1 84694 967 8

All rights reserved. Except for brief quotations in critical articles or reviews, no part of this
book may be reproduced in any manner without prior written permission from the publishers.

The rights of Carole J. Obley as author have been asserted in accordance with the Copyright,
Designs and Patents Act 1988.

A CIP catalogue record for this book is available from the British Library.

Design: Stuart Davies

Printed and bound by CPI Group (UK) Ltd, Croydon, CR0 4YY

We operate a distinctive and ethical publishing philosophy in all
areas of our business, from our global network of authors to
production and worldwide distribution.

CONTENTS

To the One Eternal Spirit;
And to those souls on earth and in spirit who illuminate the
truth of love.

Acknowledgments

I offer heartfelt appreciation to the following individuals for their contribution to my life and to this book:

Clients, both near and far, who have connected with me with the intent of gaining peace, reassurance and forgiveness. I sincerely hope that my sessions, in some small way, have helped to ease your burdens and offered you validation of continued love on your journey;

My family and friends whose unconditional support of my pathway means the world to me;

My fiancé Jeffrey Hanlin, for his daily nurturing, inspiration and unconditional love;

My dear, longtime friend Alice Teeters, for her unwavering belief in me and my work;

All of those who have come to my workshops and message programs who seek the Light;

My editor, Gina Mazza, for her professionalism, diligent efforts and kind, expert guidance;

And to my beloved spirit guides, teachers and angels who have never given up on helping me navigate through life.

PREFACE

When I began doing professional readings in the late 1990s, I had no inkling that my work would profoundly alter my perceptions about life, or did I anticipate that it would put me in touch with numerous people through the media who I could help with my abilities. At the time, I certainly had no intention to write about the people I read for, the life-changing inspiration from the spirit world that came through during these sessions or the healing that resulted from them. Truth be told, I was just grateful for the opportunity to do a couple of readings a week when I wasn't working at another part-time job that paid my living expenses. In those days, I often thought about giving up mediumship to pursue a "real" career. An intense, unexplainable awareness that I was somehow called to do this work was the single motivating factor that kept me on this path, which has become as "real" a career as any other.

Today, 15 years later, I've lost count of the thousands of readings I've done for people from numerous walks of life and various cultures. Through the years, I've been a guest on numerous radio shows and interviewed for many newspaper articles. I've stood in front of hundreds of people doing gallery-style readings. During the last decade, I've written two books, taught workshops and produced recorded materials about the spiritual realms, spirit communication, metaphysics and healing. In the process, I've experienced my own personal spiritual awakenings and emotional ups and downs, and have been blessed beyond measure.

In my second book, *I'm Still with You: True Stories of Healing Grief Through Spirit Communication*, I wanted to show how people who came to me for sessions were positively transformed during the grieving process by hearing from deceased loved ones. Over the years, one consistent theme has emerged repeatedly during private sessions: healing—in whatever form it takes—for those who hear from the other side. I believe that mediumship at its best is a powerful vehicle for grief resolution and spiritual growth. Moreover, I've observed firsthand how it bridges the gap between people and deceased loved ones by giving voice to and healing unfinished emotional issues. This book is a continuation of the journey into the healing aspect of my work, as it focuses on various emotional connections between people and their loved ones in spirit and the exploration of those relationships.

To give readers a genuine portrayal of spirit communication, I attempt to describe on the following pages what I experience during sessions in my role as medium, the specific emotional components that come up during readings and the spiritual significance of relationships. Chapter Two explores what I call the *Big Picture* provided by those in spirit and how it helps us gain a fresh, higher perspective of our lives beyond our personalities. In the final chapter of this first section, I offer insights about commonly asked questions concerning the spirit world, dream communication and earthbound spirits.

Part Two documents selected sessions with people in which the themes of forgiveness, guilt, uncertainty, fear and grief were highlighted. It also contains transcripts of sessions in which death was untimely, tragic or unexpected, as well as life lessons between clients and their loved ones. To maintain the integrity of the communications, I have transcribed the words directly from my recordings with no embellishment of meaning and with minimal editing. These stories are about real people who have in some way struggled with coming to terms with emotional issues around the death of their loved one. My hope is that you find peace, reassurance and comfort for your own life by reading them.

A book on healing is of little value unless readers recognize that the ability to heal resides within the perfection of their own souls. To help you do so, I share insights from my own intimate work in gaining spiritual awareness, moving beyond self-limiting thoughts and developing a personal connection to the higher spiritual realms in Part Three. I include methods that I have successfully used and taught to others, which (hopefully) can serve as inspiring guideposts for your unique experience.

Remember that while consulting with a reputable medium has tremendous value, you alone hold the key to spiritual awareness and healing through focusing your intent to invite it into your life. No one else can give this to you or take it away. The pure, true essence of who you are is who you have *always* been: a divine soul. No matter how long you have suffered with whatever life has presented to you, the truth is that the past has absolutely no power over you. Healing is right here, right now, in the present moment. May your path be guided by the One Light of Spirit.

cjo

February 2012

PART ONE:

SPIRITUAL PASSAGES

One

Matters of Life and Death

The boundaries which divide life from death
are at best shadowy and vague.
Who shall say where one ends and the other begins?
Edgar Alan Poe

I open my office door and greet Sandy, a petite woman with short, brown hair and glasses who appears to be in her forties. She radiates a pleasant demeanor and friendly smile, yet I immediately sense a vague, underlying sadness within her. As we chat casually about the recent snowstorm that had blanketed our area, she settles into the chair across from mine. I sit down, turn on my tape recorder and say the familiar prayer I've used thousands of times when doing readings for people who have come to me to hear from deceased loved ones:

Father-Mother God, Infinite Divine Spirit;
We give thanks for the multitude of blessings in our lives;
We give thanks for the guidance, direction and healing we are about to receive;
I ask for the highest and best for Sandy;
I call on her guides, teachers, angels and loved ones in spirit. Amen.

Focusing my attention within, I silently observe and listen to what I am sensing. In seconds, I am impressed by the presence of a male spirit who presents himself as much younger than Sandy.

"A younger male energy is here," I begin. "This must be a son or nephew to you. He makes me feel as if he is who you wanted to hear from today. Do you understand?"

Sandy's pleasant demeanor abruptly changes. Tears spill from her eyes. She draws in her breath and gasps, "Yes. It's my son."

I tune in to receive the young man's feelings and thoughts. I feel a faint fuzziness in my head, a sensation that I perceive when a spirit used alcohol or drugs before death. In this way, the young man communicates to me that addiction was a primary cause of his passing. Stepping forward in my mind's eye, he points his hands at his chest—my sign during readings that a spirit is taking personal responsibility in some way for his passing. He also impresses me with the first letters of his name: J-O. I relay all of this to Sandy.

"Yes, that's all true about Josh," she whispers.

The young man continues to give me impressions about himself and his life.

"He gives me feelings that his emotional and mental states were very confused before he died. You warned him about his lifestyle but he ignored your advice. He says he didn't mean to hurt you and that you were always there for him. Do you understand? You were there in all the ways a mother should be but you could not control his life. He made choices that were not the best for him. He says he's sorry for that."

Listening intently, Sandy dabs her eyes with a tissue and nods.

I deliver several other evidentiary messages about the young man's life, both of which Sandy confirms. A few minutes pass while she absorbs what I am saying. Each time she validates a message I give, fresh tears stream down her cheeks. I reach out and offer her another tissue.

"He is showing me question marks around his passing. It means there are circumstances about his death that are unanswered, at least in your mind. You are not at peace."

"Yes, that's true. The police still have his belongings and they just don't seem to care about who he got the drugs from that took his life. I can't let that or anything else about his death go. I lay awake at night and think about what happened to Josh. Over and over I think I didn't do enough to help him. How can I ever forgive myself?" she sobs.

I have shared a similar intimate emotional space with other individuals countless times before in sessions, although my response is always intuitively tailored to fit the specific needs of each client. To remain objective and effective while delivering messages, I cannot allow myself to be emotionally drawn into the communication taking place, yet I offer compassion when it is needed. In this case, I reach out and take Sandy's hands in mine.

"You must realize that your son made the choice to take drugs. No matter how much we'd like to believe we can save others, even our children, the truth is that we cannot. We are only responsible for our own life. Coming to terms with that will help you accept the circumstances of your son's death and allow you to heal."

"But I should have done more to help him," Sandy argues between sobs. "He struggled with drug abuse for a few years before this happened. I should have spent more time trying to get him to go back to counseling. Then maybe this wouldn't have happened. Now what can I do?"

A comforting, intuitive message comes to me. "You're in a support group, Compassionate Friends, which helps people who have lost children. Your son says that through this group you will help others who are hurting. He says that you'll also come to terms with the fact that you didn't cause his death, that he is the one who made the choice to take drugs, despite being warned. He is really emphasizing that. Do you understand the spiritual meaning of your relationship with your son?"

Sandy looks down at her lap before answering. "No. And maybe if I did, it would bring me peace. I mean, Josh was only 20, with his whole life in front of him. Why would this happen?"

"He's saying that he taught you about compassionate detachment and forgiveness. His addiction presented you with the opportunity to love him, but you needed to learn how to detach from trying to control him and the disease. You now have the choice to learn from his death, forgive him and yourself, and help others."

Sandy takes a deep breath. "I know that in my head but not my heart. I do feel better after hearing that from him, though. I think about him all the time. I'm afraid I won't ever be with my child again and that scares me. Most of all, I miss him and feel I've gotten signs from him. Is it possible for me to open my own line of communication with him? Is there a way you can teach me to do that?"

I sense that hope is beginning to penetrate through the dark, oppressive grief that had invaded Sandy's life. "Yes. We'll discuss that in another session, when you are feeling more at peace with his passing. For now, know that you couldn't have changed the outcome of your son's death, despite all of your efforts to save him. He is the one who chose his pathway. I suggest you meditate on forgiveness of yourself and him. It's very important that you connect with the core of who you are as a spiritual being. That is the anchor that will help you during painful times."

The reading transitions into a discussion of other areas of Sandy's life -her work and a possible upcoming move. A short time later, I close the session. After thanking me profusely, Sandy is on her way. I am grateful I play a small part in her newfound awareness of herself in the wake of a tragic event. The spiritual seeds have been planted. It is up to her to nurture them and watch them blossom.

Is it possible to resolve painful emotions about loved ones who have passed into spirit? If we can, by what means do we do it? Does the other side help us in our times of need? From a spiritual perspective, is there a higher purpose to tragic circumstances, such as a child's passing or the murder or suicide of a parent, sibling or friend? In my role as medium through many sessions,

I have been blessed to gain direct insight about these questions from souls in spirit. At times, these insights have been startling, compelling and direct; in other cases, they have been delivered with a humorous, lighthearted twist from the communicating spirit's point of view. In some instances, I have been filled with an overwhelming sense of love coming from the other side that I attempt to put into words for clients. The unifying factor in all of the communication with my clients is spiritual understanding to grow beyond suffering.

Although they are different in terms of the client's age, relationship, economic status and many other factors, readings that I've done share one simple, common denominator: people want to feel better than before the session took place. That is their sole purpose in coming to see me in the first place. Please understand that it is not me who makes the "sitter" (as I refer to them) feel at peace or experience emotional release from painful, unresolved attachments to the past; it is the ever-present, encompassing connection with Spirit within them that heals. (Spirit with a capital "s" refers to the divine life force within each of us, as opposed to "spirit", which refers to the individual souls who have crossed into the spirit world.)

Through years of doing readings and my own personal spiritual studies, I've discovered that the *only* way we heal grief, release negative attachments to the past and grow beyond self-depreciating emotions is by making a connection with and developing a relationship with the spark of the Divine within. It is the way out of misery and the beacon of light that guides us to ultimate freedom of being. It is the calm at the eye of the storm.

How the Process Works

If this book is the first exposure you've had to mediumship or spirit communication, you probably need a straightforward, clear description of how it works. If you would like to know more about the specific mechanics of communicating with the spirit world, I recommend that you read my second book, *I'm Still with You*, which explains the process in detail and how I receive information. For now, I will highlight only the really important things involved to help you understand the dynamics that operate in readings. I describe these in the clearest way possible, considering the limitations of language when it comes to defining energetic phenomena such as mediumship. If you've received readings, you already know what the experience is like. My goal is to give you a picture of what is going on during readings from my perspective as medium.

Let me begin by saying that, in my humble opinion, the main purpose of doing readings as a conduit, a bridge between those in the spirit world and those who come to sessions, is healing. Humility is required when one is bringing healing to individuals. Healing has always been my primary intent, which I believe makes all the difference in the world as far as what people take with them when they leave my office or hang up the phone after a session. That being the case, I affirm this intention at the beginning of each session with a prayer for the highest, best experience for the client. Then I let go of my own expectations about the session. I admit that I am not immune to falling into the same "expectation" trap as some clients do before readings. In fact, expectations about a reading from the medium or client can dramatically affect the process in a negative way. I'll explain more about that in other chapters.

Since healing is the primary aim of mediumship, it's important to understand exactly what it means to heal. Like most spiritual truths, the meaning is uncomplicated: to heal is to awaken to one's true, pure essence as Spirit. This means we recognize that life's circumstances are events that happen to us, but are *not* us. Our true, real essence is pure and untouched by any outside influence. The fact that we can rise above (so to speak) tragic or painful events indicates that we exist independently of them. We, as Spirit, are never diminished or limited by what happens to us. Relinquishing the illusion (false belief) that the past holds any power over us is the point where all healing begins.

Prior to readings, I typically know next to nothing about clients— often the client's first name and that's it. I certainly don't know who they want to hear from in spirit. In fact, it is preferable that a reputable medium knows nothing about clients' lives before readings. (Exceptions are people I've done more than one reading for and, on occasion, those who blurt out to me who they expect to hear from.) Although a few people over the years have asserted that I research people's family and personal histories on the Internet, I assure you that I do not. I also do not need to hold an object belonging to the person in spirit (this is called "psychometry") in order to tune in. Nor do I use photos of the deceased. All of the communication coming from those in spirit is received through my mind and inner senses (which I'll explain shortly.)

After I say my opening prayer, I turn on the "switch" that opens the door to the spirit world. Yes, it's that quick. I like to think of it as raising an internal antenna and flipping it to the "on" position. I've "tuned the radio" to the frequency of the nonphysical world. I then fine-tune it to the specific spirits that are coming in on the wave of the sitter in front of me or, in the case of phone readings, on the other end of the connection. I use my internal antenna as a scope of sorts to feel who is coming in to speak. What happens next is important for you to understand.

The basic set-up of a reading consists of my first offering clients specific information that validates the identity of the communicating spirit, and secondly, delivery of "the goods" from those spirits—meaning, messages of confirmation, guidance and healing. I wish I could tell you that there are hard and fast rules for the way spirits communicate (despite my asking them to) but this is hardly the case. They will say what they want to and it's up to me to interpret it and pass it along. Think of my role as an audience member in a game of charades, where no verbal language is allowed. Most times, I get the message; sometimes, I miss the mark due to my own misinterpretation.

The main challenges I face as a medium are removing myself as much as possible from my own personal mind and interpreting the messages correctly. In both cases, there is room for error. I increase the chances of giving a successful reading by meditating before every reading and describing what I am seeing, sensing and hearing as precisely as I can to clients. In honesty, however, mishaps can still occur. Spirit communication does not conform to the standard left-brain rules of logic and science since the medium is receiving the information through thoughts and feelings; yet there continue to be ongoing, scientific experiments on mediumship that prove its validity. (For more on this, a good internet resource can be found at veritas.arizona.edu)

Once I zero in on spirits who are present (male or female, young or old), I begin to receive psychic impressions about them. These usually include the placement of the spirit in relationship to the client. For example, if a spirit is the client's mother, I will sense or see them over the right shoulder of the client (the maternal lineage) and slightly behind them to indicate one generation removed. At times, this can be confusing from my vantage point since aunts could also be in this position since they are from the same generation as a mother. In these cases, I mentally ask spirits for more information to validate their identity. I conduct a silent, mental interview during which I ask them their names, how they passed, the nature of their personalities and what they did for a living. I ask them to show me a distinguishing characteristic about themselves. I then convey this information to clients.

Other impressions are forthcoming once I make the energetic link. Souls in spirit use these details about their earthly lives because during readings, their consciousness becomes temporarily focused in physical reality. Thus, they identify with or remember the physical conditions they experienced during life and death. Once identity has been established, I mentally ask for messages to give to clients. That is where the real punch of the reading lies as far as the healing aspect of mediumship. As you read the stories in this book, you will see how people's lives can be remarkably changed and healed as a result of hearing from those in spirit who communicate messages of love, forgiveness and hope.

I receive these messages through the inner or soul senses of clairaudience (hearing), clairvoyance (seeing) and clairsentience (feeling.) Each sense blends with the others, forming a tapestry or impression that I interpret and put into language for sitters. During the reading, I obtain feedback by asking sitters if they understand the message or by asking for a simple "yes", "no" or "I don't know." I usually do not want clients to expound on messages I give until the end of the reading. I ask people to not reveal details to me before those in spirit do. Otherwise, I can't make use of those particular facts for validation.

That's it, as far as the process goes. An easy way for you to understand how the communication during readings takes place is to think of a triangle in which each point represents either a receiver or a communicator of information: souls in the spirit world, medium and client. If all points are open, the energetic dynamic that takes place should flow from point A to B to C in a circular manner. If any are closed or clogged in some way, the communication will not take place or will be muddled. I've discovered that the number one variable (over which I have no control) is the receptivity of clients. I will discuss this in the next section.

A word needs to be added about how it's possible to do readings over the phone with people who are often many miles away. The answer is that the communication is energy-based, coming from the spiritual, non-physical realms and is therefore not affected or restrained by physical distance. I've connected with people from other continents with positive results. Souls (both on earth and in spirit) can transcend physical boundaries through connecting on a soul level. For those who still have doubts, consider the power of prayer, which also operates effectively on this same energetic level of awareness. It's a good analogy, and substantial scientific research has verified the healing power of prayer.

A question that clients frequently bring up is the relevancy of time and relationship to communicating spirits. I'll explain by using an example from a reading I did recently for Nancy, whose great aunt Katy (her father's aunt) came through by name and how she passed.

For a few minutes after I connected with her aunt (who impressed me with her name), Nancy insisted that she knew no one in the family by that name. The aunt's personality was strong and I sensed she was not going away until she was recognized. So I persisted by saying that Nancy did indeed know someone in the family by that name. Finally, her face lit up and she said, "My dad had an aunt named Katy but she died over 20 years ago and I barely knew her. Why would she come through?"

I told her I didn't know why but she clearly wanted Nancy to acknowledge her and her dad's side of the family. I explained to her that there is no time in the spirit world and, obviously, her great aunt wanted to greet her. Later in the reading, it was revealed that Nancy's paternal side was having a family reunion in a few months. This was likely what her aunt Katy wanted to validate.

From my vantage point during readings, there's an entire story, impression by impression, going on in my head that I must "translate" into spoken language. It's all incredibly real and vivid to me. Language can be limiting (especially when feelings come in) to convey the story that the other side is telling me. I compare it to what Dorothy must have felt like when she stepped out of the bleakness of her tornado-ravaged home into the Land of Oz. Remember how *The Wizard of Oz* depicted the contrast between Dorothy's everyday life in Kansas and the Land of Oz by changing the film from black and white to color when she stepped over the rainbow? That's what it's like for me when I communicate with the unseen world of energy from the spirit world: vividly colorful and captivatingly alive.

How Spirit Communication Heals

As I mentioned earlier, the main intent I hold for clients during sessions is that of healing, emotional release and spiritual understanding. I am no more in control of the outcome of sessions than I am in changing the weather. That is up to the free will of clients and the willingness of the other side to come through at the "appointed" time. I simply hold that intention as the facilitator of a "family reunion." My job is to receive and deliver the information as clearly as possible. There are several key factors that determine the extent to which healing occurs and that directly affect the success of the reading: the readiness and openness of people to receive healing, their present spiritual consciousness and my effectiveness in interpreting the information from the spirit world. If one factor is strong and the other(s) weak, the reading loses some of its healing power. Long ago, I wondered if I could somehow improve the odds of creating a stronger link with sitters. The answer came through years of experience. Here's what happened:

I discovered that if I asked people to meditate and write questions they wanted to explore before coming to a session, the strength of the reading was greatly improved. In the triangle example I gave earlier, the greatest variable is the openness of clients. Meditation helps to widen the channels of communication by creating awareness of Spirit within. This awareness is the source and bond with those in spirit. In essence, the link is made between those in the physical world and those in spirit before the reading takes place. Preparation of questions about areas of concern also helps since it provides intent to those in spirit. For example: *I'd like help with coming to peace with how you passed. What happened to your body before you died? Could you shed light on that?* or *Can you help me to understand what you were feeling before you took your life? Who are you with in spirit?* I've read for people who meditate and write questions before sessions and, believe me, they get far more from sessions than those who don't.

Spiritual consciousness means the awareness of oneself as Spirit, the divine life force. I can't put it any simpler than that. If we believe that our identity lies solely in the material, physical realm, we do not see the truth of who we are as spiritual beings. This is the domain of skepticism, the belief that if something cannot be proven by rational science or the five physical senses, it doesn't exist. I am not suggesting that people be open to anything and everything that comes along. It's healthy and advisable to use discernment when having readings, especially when it comes to choosing a genuine medium in the first place. But if people do not have spiritual consciousness, they have not yet opened the door to the higher guidance and healing that is possible through the invisible realms of spirit. Their beliefs may dictate that the human form is more important than the soul residing within—if the soul is even acknowledged. Or if they do recognize the soul, they may believe it is not possible or morally right (according to their religion) to communicate with those who have passed. The more aware we are of the reality of our physical interconnectedness with the non-physical world, the more spiritually awake we become. Optimally, mediumship should offer the philosophy of harmonious living in accordance with natural laws and the understanding of one's life from a spiritual perspective.

The third factor—my ability to interpret the information—can be affected by my own personal frame of reference, my physical and emotional state and plain human error on my part. I do my best to control each of these variables by mediating before every reading, putting my personal opinions and expectations aside and staying as physically and emotionally balanced as I can. Still mix-ups occur, especially in the case of clairvoyance, which necessitates my describing to clients what I am seeing. I am honest with people when I tell them I can't account for messages that don't make sense at the time of the reading because few messages ever make sense to me as the impartial channel of communication. If something doesn't "ring a bell" with clients during readings, chances are it will later. I've received many follow-up calls and emails from people who validate "unclaimed" messages from earlier readings.

When all three of the above factors are in place and operating, the reading packs an incredible healing wallop. As a facilitator of sessions, I see this happen when I intuitively sense clients' emotions shift, or witness them cry, laugh and utter sighs of relief. The healing continues long after the reading and I often encourage people to support the process by engaging in daily spiritual practices such as meditation, breath-awareness and prayer.

So how can one reading make such a dramatic difference in the life of someone who has suffered for years from guilt, for example, over not having done enough to help a deceased loved one before passing? By hearing that same loved one communicate that they are aware of the guilt and that it didn't affect their love for the person. How can years of grief over having an argument with a loved one just prior to death be healed? By hearing "I'm sorry we had a falling-out before I passed. I forgive you." I've read for people who have carried hurt feelings towards a loved one for many years. Despite the length of time and the magnitude of the wound, the emotional debris of the past is swept away and transformed into spiritual understanding when the spiritual light within a client is switched on.

I have never promoted mediumship as the be-all and cure-all

for healing, nor do I advocate that it replace the natural process of grieving or psychotherapy. Rather, I feel it is *one* tool among many on the pathway of healing relationships with those who have passed, as well as for growing spiritually. When I first started doing readings, my spirit guides (the souls on the other side who help me with mediumship) told me that I need to maintain integrity in the field. I've never forgotten that. With that foremost in my mind, I've turned people away who I sense need to go to therapy instead of having a reading with me, as well as those who I felt could become dependent on sessions. In other cases, I've suggested that people go through the initial stages of grieving first then come to see me. To this day, I have not regretted pointing someone towards the best avenue of growth.

Healing and the Present Moment

As human beings in physical bodies, we operate in the context of time: past, present and future. In the spirit world, there is no concept of time, only awareness of "now." Our spiritual essence operates in this same capacity of immediacy. This is where the potential for healing lies—in the present moment. The past and future—constructs of our human mind—are not available to us except through memory and projection. On the other hand, the present moment is always right here, right now, ever fresh. It is within this context that we can make a choice to let go of that which is no longer serving our highest good. In an instant, we can choose to release old wounds rooted in the past, feel joy and experience the lightness of our own being through forgiveness.

During readings, communication with those in spirit happens in the present moment and so lends itself directly to the opportunity for emotional release of the past. The length of time that emotional wounds have been held doesn't matter; the chance to release them is always fresh and available. Here's an example:

I recently did a phone reading with Laura, who wanted

insight about her career. Midway during the reading, she asked if I could connect with her relatives in spirit. I focused in on an older female's presence appearing on Laura's right side (the maternal lineage.)

"She impresses me that she passed from congestion in the lung area, probably pneumonia," I conveyed.

On the other end of the phone, Laura began to cry. "Yes, it's my mom. That's how she died. She had pneumonia."

I continued with a straightforward message. "She says it's no one's fault that she died this way."

Laura's crying turned into sobs of recognition. "Oh, my God! I can't believe this! For years, my brother and sisters and I have felt really guilty at not having done more to help Mom before she died. We arrived at the hospital late on the day she was admitted and decisions about her care had already been made by other family members who were there. Since then, we've felt really bad that we weren't there to try and save her. It means so much to hear Mom say we didn't do anything wrong!"

I have no doubt that this simple message from her mom changed Laura's perception forever, freeing her to move beyond unresolved guilt.

The other side knows about our feelings, both positive and painful, and they want us to live "debt free" from the past, so to speak. On top of that, they want us to be happy in the moment. I've come to realize that by delivering messages of healing, those in spirit also heal themselves. The circle of love is eternal. Souls on the other side have seen what I call the BP—the Big Picture, which we'll investigate in the next chapter.

If you are reading this book because you want to heal relationships with someone in spirit, I urge you to begin the process today, in the present moment. The first and most important step is your willingness to release, for it is entirely your choice to move beyond the past and grasp the pure potential of renewal that is happening right now, in this very moment.

The Truth Resides in Your Soul

In addition to doing readings, I've spent many years studying and teaching metaphysical spirituality, through which I've come to understand and, more importantly, *experience* certain spiritual truths. As these concepts unveiled themselves to me, I discovered more missing puzzle pieces fall into place in my quest to improve my life. On my pathway of being both student and teacher, I've met many others who've also resonated with the experiences that I am about to share. My hope in sharing them is that you will likewise benefit, especially in knowing yourself and others as Spirit, the spark of the divine. I'll address several of the more common themes that I've encountered in my journey.

The Soul's Purpose for Coming into Physical Form

The single reason we choose to come into the physical world from the dimension of spirit is for our soul's growth. As is often the case with spiritual matters, this truth can best be stated by making a paradoxical statement: We come to earth to remember who we are by discovering who we are *not*. How can this be?

At some point in time during our lives, most of us get diverted or lost from our true identity as Spirit by giving too much focus to our ego—or, the dimension of our personality-self in our physical body. We are easily lulled into accepting that all there is to life is what we can detect through our physical senses and the outside world. We allow this limited perception of ourselves and the world to take precedence over our spiritual essence. Experiencing life from this unbalanced position causes us to suffer when that physical reality changes, deteriorates or falls away completely, such as in the loss of a job, a financial crisis, serious illness, divorce or the death of a loved one. These are what I call "wake-up calls"—compelling, life-altering events and circumstances that present opportunities for developing a deeper spiritual awareness. In fact, wake-up calls can be significant catalysts in profound spiritual awakening precisely because they cause us to suffer, usually by the removal or change of something or someone in our physical reality. Depending on our attachment to that external thing or person, the resulting experience of suffering is the gateway to a fresh awareness of our true identity as Spirit, the eternal and unchangeable.

So how can the physical world help us to realize our spiritual essence as a divine soul? If we first accept that the physical world is transient by nature, we can anchor ourselves more firmly by trusting that our internal spiritual essence is unchangeable, permanent and eternal. That is why our souls have come to experience all of the contrast that third dimensional reality offers. Pain and pleasure, evil and good, having and not having are teaching vehicles for us to remember that our spiritual essence exists beyond these contrasts of being, which happen *to* us, but are *not* us. We find out who we are by experiencing who we are not.

When we awaken through spiritual awareness, we release suffering to a large extent and see meaning in life through service to others, which is its own reward. The more we give, the more our own soul is nourished. In our own unique way, we hopefully leave the world a better place than before we were born.

The Spiritual Evolution of Your Soul

Over the years, the concept of reincarnation has come up many times in my work. People have asked me if I believe that we come back to earth in other lifetimes and if we have been here before. My response is that I do not believe in reincarnation; rather, I *know* it is true. To me, believing in something implies a mental construct that is thought to be true but may not have been solidly proven. Through doing thousands of readings, I have had the experience of seeing that we do indeed come into physical form many times. From my standpoint, there is no question about it.

When I first started doing readings, scenes, images and

impressions would appear to me above a client's left shoulder. In short order, I realized that this psychic information was revealing itself as energy from people's past experiences. Interestingly, when I share it with clients, they usually validate it in some way. (For example, I saw an image of a client as a farmer who lived in New England in a past life, and he confirmed that he loved to garden, had a green thumb and had always felt inexplicably drawn to buy farmland in the New England area even though he didn't live there). Often I'll be shown the roots of unresolved past life emotional issues—guilt, grief or addictions, for instance—which clients subsequently validate as being true in their lives now; the problem manifests again to be balanced and healed. This (if properly dealt with) releases the karma, the unfinished business from before.

I mention reincarnation because it is the vehicle through which we evolve spiritually. The reality of souls coming into physical form many times over is, at the very least, intriguing. Every so often, I meet with people who want to explore their past lives purely out of curiosity, not for healing purposes. Aside from the entertainment value of knowing who we were (most of us have not been famous; quite the opposite is true), recognizing reincarnation as the soul's repeated experiences in the physical realm helps us to understand ourselves as constantly evolving spiritual beings. We have all experienced birth, life and death many times in the never-ending spiral of our soul's journey.

Each time we come into physical form, memories of past experiences are temporarily blocked from our perception to allow focus on the current life. Our soul retains experiences from lifetime to lifetime and these energetic imprints are stored in the Akashic Records—or, nonphysical chronicles of souls' experiences from the beginning of time. They can be accessed through past-life regression therapy (a form of hypnosis), by studying our astrological natal chart or through readings with mediums who are sensitive at tuning into them. (To learn more about the

Akashic Records, see my first book, *Embracing the Ties That Bind: Connecting with Spirit*.)

The Karma of Relationships

In its simplest definition, karma means cause and effect. What we sow, we reap. In a spiritual sense, it is neither good nor bad; it is what we build and subsequently balance each time we incarnate to remember who we are as divine beings. Relationships are teaching vehicles that show us what needs to be healed within ourselves. We may have positive karma with another in that the relationship is relatively tension-free and harmonious. In these cases, the person complements our inherent good qualities. The energy between the two souls rolls along smoothly. More commonly, we have unbalanced karma within ourselves that is being mirrored to us by another and vice versa. This is precisely why we have entered into relationship with another, although we usually remain unaware of it. It is primarily through the experiences of tension and difficulty that we grow; in other words, no pain, no gain. This is not always the case but is frequently true. Parents, children, spouses, friends and employers have agreed to be in our lives to help our souls advance in some way, and we have done the same. These are what I call *soul connections*, those relationships which we have agreed to explore for purposes of both souls' growth.

Before we can embark on healing emotional connections with passed loved ones, we must understand that on a soul level, most relationships we have with others that involve an emotional connection are indeed karmic soul agreements we've made with them before physical incarnation. In my experience, rarely do we understand those specific lessons until well after the fact. It may be years before we understand what we gained from having an abusive parent or an unloving spouse, for example. Because karma is energetically-based, rarely are we consciously aware of it. We "play" it out largely unconsciously. We may have to go back into spirit ourselves before we are shown the full implications of relationships.

Indicators that point to karmic themes in life often show up in the repetition of patterns we experience in relationships over a number of years, or we may have several intense experiences in a relatively short period of time that emphasize a particular theme. I believe this is the case when people have several loved ones pass within a short span of time or have difficult circumstances such as financial problems, job loss, divorce or illness that happen all at once. Confronting crisis and emotional pain requires us to accept the inherent fairness and divine balance of life, then forgive, let go and move forward. It may take months or years for us to gain perspective about how challenging circumstances have fueled our spiritual growth. In all cases, we must trust that the infinite wisdom of Spirit is always working for our greatest good.

Acceptance—the initial step in healing emotional issues— means that we no longer resist *what is*. We come to terms with reality as it is now presented to us. Note that I use the word "now." I believe that being in present-time awareness is the single deciding factor in moving beyond suffering and onto the pathway of healing. As you will see in Section Two, people come to me for readings carrying unresolved emotions that are rooted in the past. Many people want things to be different than they are, not realizing that the only way to feel better is to change their perspective *now* about what has happened in the past. That change is only available in the present, since the past no longer exists. Total acceptance of painful emotions and the past releases resistance and begins the healing process in present time, the focal point of healing. This moves us out of suffering and into peace.

Understanding relationships from a karmic viewpoint means that we accept ourselves and others as both students and teachers in life. We acknowledge that even though the lessons can be challenging and we don't fully understand them, we are connected to others for spiritual growth. The karma contained within relationships contributes to the spiritual evolution of both souls in the continual, unfolding expression of the divine spark within each. If we don't resist the experience, working through difficulties within relationships helps us to see ourselves more clearly by cultivating the soil of our spiritual essence.

Prior Connections Between Souls

Have you felt as if you've known certain people in your life before your current association with them? Past life memories (and current ones) stored in the subconscious mind can be recalled through not only past life regression but our own intuition. Although we may not know the exact circumstances of our prior ties, we have vague feelings of familiarity about them nonetheless. I've encountered many people who have also had psychic connections with others through dreams, feelings and precognition.

In the current lifetime, both souls have come back together for further growth. There is "unfinished business" from the prior connection that led each to one another. I like to think of this karmic connection as an electrical charge within souls that magnetically, unconsciously draws them together. The circular nature of our life as souls, often referred to as the "wheel of karma," means that we return to the physical world to continue to evolve through experiences here. Relationships play a vital role in this process as mirroring vehicles for the personality of each person. Through this process, refinement of the personality of each takes place. This allows more of the soul to shine forth without the infringement of the ego.

Healing soul connections means that we change or release the charge between us and another. Is it possible to do this even if the other person is unaware of our intent or is not in favor of it for some reason? I believe so since changing the energy of one person in the relationship necessarily changes the core energy of the relationship. Here are two simple analogies illustrating this dynamic: Imagine being on one end of a see-saw with a person on the other end. If you get off the see-saw, the entire balance of the unit changes. Now envision holding a rope and playing tug of war with a dog. What would happen if you let go of your end of the rope? Minus the possibility of injuries occurring in both of these examples, you can easily see how one person's letting go changes the flow of the interaction.

Sometimes, one soul has agreed to lead the way, in a spiritual sense, for the other. In these cases, that soul's spiritual consciousness within the relationship is the catalyst for both souls' growth. Since relationship dynamics are hard to pinpoint when we're engaged in them, forgiveness (letting go of perceived hurts) is the way to go as far as healing is concerned. Staying rooted in the past by holding resentments, anger and other negative emotions will necessitate future relearning of the same lessons. We'll take a closer look at soul agreements in the next chapter.

Forgiveness as the Cornerstone of Healing

Throughout this book, you will read numerous references to the power of forgiveness in healing and spiritual self-empowerment. In all the years that I've been a medium and spiritual teacher, I've come to understand that forgiveness is not only vital to the process of healing grief, relationships and painful circumstances in life, it is the core ingredient of spiritual growth. So what exactly does it mean to forgive? My definition is simple: to let go of the past. Once we let go, we can be fully present in the now, where all healing occurs. Engaging in forgiveness gives us the opportunity to start over with a fresh, clean slate.

In my earlier books, I wrote about my recovery from substance abuse and how it ultimately (and surprisingly) led me into my work as a medium. During those confusing and frightening days of early recovery, I read many books to find spiritual direction, solace and hope. One of my favorites was *Each Day a New Beginning* by the Hazelton Foundation, which offered inspiring thoughts and prayers for each day of the year. Every morning, shortly after waking, I would read the day's passage and see how I could apply it to my life. The key concept put forth in most of the passages was that each day of recovery from substance abuse offers us a chance to start over without the weight of the past. The spiritual light of that simple wisdom stuck with me and got me through many dark moments over the years.

The same is true concerning our spiritual growth through healing our relationships. There is no time like the present to let go. Clinging to the past and reliving resentment, anger, guilt and fear keeps us trapped in a prison of our own making, one in which we are victims. Forgiveness frees us by allowing us to start over with a renewed awareness of Spirit within.

During sessions, I've recommended to clients that they practice forgiveness in the midst of emotional turmoil over unresolved pain about loved ones' deaths. Occasionally, people argue that they find it impossible to forgive the wrongs that they perceive have been done to them or family members. I've discovered one of two beliefs is operating in these cases: people are not *willing* to let go of the past due to the tenacity of their own ego or they don't understand the real meaning of forgiveness. In some cases, both are true.

Forgiveness does not mean that we are condoning the perceived wrongs that someone has done to us; rather, it means that we decide to no longer carry the burden of negative feelings about a person or circumstance. Letting go means just that: allowing the heavy burden of resentment, guilt, anger, hurt and fear to fall away from our mind and heart. When we turn these over to Spirit, we relinquish the need to continually relive the past. This is what the Bible refers to as the peace that passes all understanding.

As you read this book, my hope is that you will awaken to the innocence and perfection through which Spirit experiences you. Then you can align your vision of yourself and others to match that same purity.

Two

The Big Picture

The oak sleeps in the acorn, the bird waits in the egg, and in the highest vision of the soul, a waking angel stirs.
James Allen

What particular insights do those in spirit have to offer us? In addition to coming through in readings and providing compelling evidence of their continued existence after passing, souls on the other side have given information about what I call the Big Picture, or BP—an all encompassing, spiritually centered perspective of life and death from their vantage point in spirit. In this chapter, I highlight some of the common themes that come up during client sessions and from my metaphysical studies. As you read this, it's important to keep in mind that those in spirit have a much different perspective than we do on the physical plane. This does not mean they are somehow superior to us in a spiritual sense, only that they are able to see beyond their former human egos and personalities. In other words, they can see the BP, a greatly expanded vision of life. This wisdom is not only communicated in sessions by those whom we have known and loved in our lifetime, but also by spirit guides- souls who have agreed to help us on our life's pathway.

Souls returning to the spirit world are shown a panoramic life review that reveals the implications of choices made in the recent lifetime. From this perspective, souls can see how these choices affected both the self and others. They also see how they could have taken avenues that would have been more closely aligned with love, compassion, forgiveness or service. This expanded insight that they pass along to us helps us with challenges and difficulties on our earthly journeys.

Long ago, I noticed that in some sessions, I'd deliver information that went beyond the usual format of identification of passed loved ones and personal messages to clients. At times, these messages are given by clients' deceased loved ones and spirit guides as spiritual insights about current challenges in clients' lives. In one instance, my client Barb's mom in spirit made reference to a difficult relationship that Barb had with her dad- still alive. Her mom suggested that she focus on the positive qualities of her dad instead of his tendencies to be controlling. She added that she understood how Barb felt since she had struggled with the same issue with her husband and that by focusing on the positive, Barb would remove the "charge" from the relationship with her dad.

In other sessions, spirit guides offer wisdom about specific spiritual questions that clients have written or thought about prior to the session. On many occasions, the other side addresses these without clients even having to verbally state them. For example, guides may inspire me to deliver messages about what happens to us when we die and what happens during transition to the spirit world. As I'm giving these messages, I have no idea why I'm talking about that particular topic. Usually, clients are astonished that the information given addressed a question that they had written down before our session.

An important fact to understand is that souls on the other side are aware of our thoughts and feelings. How? Thoughts and feelings are energy and can therefore be read and interpreted, just as we read words in a book. Verbal language is one form of communication and non-verbal is another; both communicate ideas and describe states of being. In many readings I've done, spirits come through and make references to the brightness of light emanating from a person's soul. What this means is that in the spirit world, souls are able to see the relative darkness or light that shines forth from other souls, based on the intensity of energy that emanates from them. In spirit, there is no hiding one's true essence.

Developing the inner senses (as described in Chapter One) gives us the ability to tune into the world of non-physical energy. We'll explore that later. For right now, just know that beyond any doubt, your loved ones, spirit guides and angels (beings of divine light whose mission is to help humanity) are not only aware of your thoughts and feelings, they also send you loving, uplifting inspiration to help you in your life.

The One Million Dollar Question

Of all the questions that people come to sessions with, this one is the most common: *What is the purpose of my life?* I've joked that if I had a dollar for every time I've heard that, I'd be a millionaire. I direct that bit of humor at myself also since there was a time not so long ago when I went to psychics with that same question. I had no earthly idea what I was supposed to be doing with my life nor did I recognize myself as a spiritual being. I wanted all of the answers about my life neatly tied up in a beautiful, perfectly wrapped package. After many years of disappointment when that didn't pan out, I ultimately took off my rose-colored glasses and woke up to discover that my life was evolving in the direction it needed to in accordance with my spiritual awareness and not necessarily as I wanted it to, according to my ego. At the time, I didn't realize that what my soul needed to experience in terms of spiritual growth would lead to real fulfillment, not the fleeting happiness that my ego insisted on chasing. When I realized the difference and let go of my need to control outcomes, life improved.

So when clients ask about the purpose of their lives, I know first-hand how frustrating it can be to be disconnected from that awareness. In some sessions, those on the other side give reminders that the primary purpose in life is to embrace Spirit within. They see who we are as spiritual beings and how we express that in the world through outer purpose: a career, volunteer work, family or other means. Here's an example from a recent reading:

"I feel as if something is missing in my life," Debbie shares. "I'm a nurse but I feel there's something more to life. Is there something I can do to be more spiritual? Does my mom in spirit give any advice on that?"

A moment passes as I silently ask Debbie's mom this question. I immediately receive a feeling through clairsentience that I can best describe as reassurance. I convey this to Debbie.

"She says you are already meeting with your purpose by being who you are. Further, that being a nurse requires the spiritual qualities of compassion, nurturing and healing. You understand this, don't you?"

"Yes," Debbie replies. "I guess I thought there was something else I should do in addition to my work."

Debbie's mom impresses me to emphasize what I was about to say to her daughter. "You're already doing it, she says. She sees that you are coming to a deeper understanding of yourself as a spiritual being *because of* your work. She adds that you've been reading books about that and you are *exactly* where you need to be with everything. I get the sense here that she sees you in the true light of who you are, despite your doubts about not doing enough. You *are* enough and that's what counts from her spiritual vantage point."

Sometimes those on the other side will reminisce about the quality of their lives and express regrets for not having woken up to more meaningful avenues of expressing love during their lives. They want to pass these insights along to help prevent family members from making similar mistakes. Over the years, I've done dozens of readings in which the spirit communicator (usually male) regrets making work and money more important than giving love to or spending time with his family. They make reference to being a good provider for their family but spending very little time giving affection or love. These messages offer healing for both sides, as they highlight what's really important in life.

As far as life purpose is concerned, the bottom line is that we *are* enough, just as we are. Those on the other side see how brightly the light of our souls (and not our worldly accomplishments) shine.

The Other Side's View of the Spiritual Meaning of Relationships

Reuniting family members has its joys and pitfalls. I'm frequently amazed (and sometimes amused) at the family dynamics that are revealed. Because I serve as a non-biased bridge between people seen and unseen, I assume a non-judgmental, relatively detached role in the process. If I didn't, I'd be continually consumed with people's problems and feelings, which would zap my spiritual balance, making me ineffective. Those in spirit do the same; they offer a comparatively neutral perspective of life and relationships from a higher vantage point. That is, they have less ego investment than we do through our personality.

For me, one of the most fascinating topics that comes up in client sessions is why we have (or had) particular relationships — and by "why," I mean "spiritually speaking." What I've discovered is that although most people remain unaware of it, they have indeed made prior agreements with others to play particular relationship roles — be it as close friends, family members, significant others or work associates. Through my experiences, here is what I've been shown:

Before we come into the physical world, we make an assessment, with the help of our spirit guides, of what our soul needs to experience in order to evolve. We are shown what specific relationships and circumstances lend themselves to our spiritual advancement at that point in our evolution. On this basis, we choose to be in relationship with souls who become our parents, children, mates, friends, co-workers and such. After we are born, we may not consciously remember making these agreements, yet these interactions are fundamental to the blueprint of the life that our soul formed before we incarnated. On a soul level, we know what we are here to experience but we are seldom consciously aware of the specific karmic themes we have agreed to learn. I believe this is so because we need to evolve in the natural timeframe of our soul, not from our personal will, which is put forth by our egos. Relationships, the teaching mirrors for our souls, play a vital role in this.

At every turn, we are presented with the power of our free will to either follow the inner pathway of spiritual truth (the soul's expression) or succumb to the voice of the ego, which operates in a limited, narrow capacity compared to the soul. To understand this further, it's helpful to think of the ego as the "small" you and the soul as the eternal, expansive essence of who you are at your core. In many sessions, spirit guides have impressed on me that the "right" way to go in life is the pathway that leads to a closer connection with Spirit within. Choices that we make in life take us toward or away from that connection. There is no right or wrong; everything in the physical plane ultimately leads us to the reality of who we are as spiritual beings. Even so-called bad choices (mistakes) eventually lead us to a deeper connection with Spirit, although it is usually through the experience of suffering. How long it takes is up to us; our soul's awareness is timeless and takes many lifetimes to evolve.

As mentioned earlier, rarely do we know the intricacies of our chosen karma until well after the experience of having it. Even then, we're fortunate if we know one-tenth of what we're here to learn. When we return to our home in the spirit world, we are shown the blueprint from the life just lived and how well we followed its framework. This is shown in the panoramic vision I referred to earlier.

The spiritual meaning and relevance of relationships lie in

their ability to teach us soul qualities that we need to recognize within ourselves, such as harmony, cooperation, forgiveness, parience, humility, nurturing, endurance and unconditional love. The person we are in relationship with either mirrors these directly to us or shows us their contrast. In both cases, the energy of the quality is brought into sharp focus for us, front and center, for our attention. In the same way, we are mirrors for others, so we are both student and teacher in all relationships. The following illustrates this:

Kerrie, 35, had been married and divorced twice. When she came for a session, she wanted to know if her current relationship with David would be a lasting one. She distrusted his motives in their relationship. The reading revealed that Kerrie's father (still alive) was an alcoholic. All of her life, he was emotionally distant from her, showing her little love or affection. Kerrie's spirit guides pointed out that she had subconsciously, unsuccessfully tried to win her father's love through choosing men who were emotionally abusive to her. If she could somehow convert them into loving her, she could make up for her father's lack of love. Kerrie played out this painful pattern for many years, which took a huge toll on her self-worth. Finally, she entered therapy and started her emotional recovery. Still, she felt like a failure and wanted to know if David would be like the others. Her guides assured her that he was different and she was reacting out of fear from the past. They explained that if we hold a pattern in relationship for many years or lifetimes, that when the pendulum of energy begins to move to the other side of that expression, sometimes it goes too far; that is, it goes to the opposite polarity. In Kerrie's case, where she had little discretion in choosing men who would return her love, she now was fearful of opening her heart to receive love from a man who was indeed able to genuinely return that love. Her guides advised her to keep her heart open to give and receive love. After our session, Kerrie told me that the reading gave her insight and hope about her relationship. She felt prepared to release the past pain.

Sometimes a particular karmic thread played out in relationships starts generations ago and is highlighted in readings so people can recognize and heal it. In many readings, I've delivered messages from clients' great-grandparents about themes such as emotional abandonment, mental illness, substance abuse or physical and sexual abuse. The other side will show how the theme is perpetuating in the current generation. I've come to understand that this is their way of helping to heal both family members' and their own karma that was not resolved when they were alive. After crossing over, they've no doubt seen how the karmic pattern has affected all of the generations.

In life, we may encounter souls who strongly resonate with us as far as life circumstances, lessons and spiritual consciousness are concerned. These kindred souls are likely from our own *soul group*, which is comprised of souls with similar spiritual evolution. We may have come back into relationship with them to undertake an important task in the current lifetime or to learn a particular soul quality from one another. Our soul group may have members in the spirit world as well as the physical world. Sometimes, we meet with other souls with whom we've shared karma in former lives. One person may need to bring healing to the other to balance the karma. Other times, they involve beneficial contacts with others who can help us advance spiritually. Souls frequently find one another by magnetic resonance, which is the universal law of like energy attracting like energy. The coding set out in the blueprint helps with this process, yet much of it remains blocked from our conscious awareness.

I have seen how people incarnate with certain life-theme rays, which are indicative of the soul group to which they belong. "Ray" refers to a particular quality of the Divine that is being expressed from the soul. Examples of life-theme rays are healers, teachers, artists, nurturers, innovators, peacemakers and leaders, among others. Many people are a combination of several soul groups with two or more life themes. Although we share rays with others, we are capable of making a unique contribution to the world through our individual emanation of that ray. To identify your own soul group, consider what soul qualities you easily and effortlessly express. What do they reveal about your life pathway? What like-minded souls have helped you along the way?

The Other Side Helps us with Similar Life Lessons

When Theresa, 47, came to consult with me, I immediately sensed she had suffered a difficult life. Her eyes rarely met mine during the hour-long reading and I felt emotional heaviness around her entire being. The first ten minutes of our time together seemed interminable because she stared at the floor and squirmed nervously in her chair. After giving her psychic insights about her work, I asked if she wanted to hear from someone in spirit. Still gazing downward, she nodded.

At that moment, I wondered if I'd be able to give her anything more since she felt so emotionally removed from life. Could her loved ones in spirit crack the hard, defensive wall I felt around her? Finally, I began to receive impressions of an older female on her left side—the maternal line in my system of spirit identification. The woman (one generation removed from Theresa) came through by impressing me with her name. Margaret conveyed that she had passed from congestive heart failure. I relayed this information to Theresa.

"Uh- uh," she mutters.

I went into the zone of receiving more mental impressions from the woman. *Give me a message for her, please,* I say to Margaret telepathically.

Suddenly, I am startled by an infusion of images and vague sensations of physical and emotional abuse. It wasn't clear if Margaret had been the victim or if this applied to her daughter sitting in front of me. I share what I am experiencing with

Theresa.

"Your mom impresses me with abuse issues around her or you. Do you understand this?"

Theresa's subdued, detached demeanor abruptly changes. "Yeah," she responds, her voice cracking. "My mom was abused for years by my dad who used to beat her and call her names. She never had the courage to leave him. I never spoke to him after I left home at 18. He died five years ago. We were strangers by the time he died."

I listen yet continue to focus on Margaret in the spirit world. I silently ask her to give me another message for Theresa.

"She is making me feel as if your life is like hers was. Are you in an abusive relationship? If so, she wants you to leave while you still can. Do you understand what she means?"

"Yep, I do," Theresa answers, her eyes meeting mine for the first time in the session. "I've been planning to leave my boyfriend for a long time. He's always drunk and takes most of the money from my paychecks. In the past year, he hit me after he'd been drinking. Lately I've felt that Mom has been sending me thoughts about where I could go and who could help me. Is she really doing that?" Theresa asks tearfully.

"Yes. She does not want you to be condemned to a life like hers. She says you deserve better and she's helping you to realize that. She says she had no choice when she was here. She had to depend on your father to survive. You, however, *can* make a move away from this situation as soon as possible."

The reading continues with more messages from other relatives on Theresa's maternal side but judging from Theresa's reactions, none carried the emotional impact of her mom's message.

After the reading, Theresa thanks me warmly and promises to return. Her mom's loving message had penetrated the defensive exterior formed through the years of pain she had endured. It was astounding to see the transformation of this solemn, dejected woman who had walked into my office a mere hour before. My hope is that Theresa gained a significantly improved sense of herself, courtesy of her mom's continued love for her.

Theresa's story is one of many readings I've done in which deceased loved ones come through with messages about clients' similar life lessons. As I mentioned before, they see these sessions as their opportunity to help others, as well as themselves. It is up to clients whether they apply this wisdom, love and healing to their lives or not. I'm just the delivery person.

I've seen how spirit beings can be persistent in making themselves heard. Sometimes they offer the "kick in the pants" that people need to pay attention. More often than not, clients respond to these life lesson messages with something like this: "I've been feeling that way for awhile now and my dad in spirit confirmed it," or "Last week my best friend told me I need to get help for my drinking and now my brother in spirit has mentioned it." Usually, these statements are preceded by the word "funny"—meaning, "curiously." For example:

"Your dad says that you've been unhappy with your job for a long time and are thinking about leaving," I comment. "He says he wasted a lot of years doing something he didn't enjoy. He suggests that you follow through and look into something else."

"*Funny*, I've been thinking about that for a long time," the client responds. "Just the other day my buddy Bob told me his company was hiring and I should go for an interview."

Those on the other side can and do inspire us with guidance about our lives. Please note: rarely does this information hit us over the head, so to speak. Rather, it is subtly communicated through dreams, inspiration or synchronicity, which means that we encounter the same or similar messages several times in a relatively short period of time. So if you're waiting to have your mom deliver messages to you via a full-body materialization, you may be waiting for a long time. That's not to say those in spirit don't give us messages through physical means; they do.

Flashing lights and telephones, the appearance of birds, repeating numbers on clocks and license plates are examples of spirits' calling cards; but more often than not they use less obvious means. The content of messages may vary but the intent seldom does: they want us to be happy, free and live our lives in fulfillment and peace.

The BP and What Really Matters

Earlier, I mentioned that client's expectations about whom and what will come through can affect the success of readings. In short, if people hold preconceived notions about who will or should communicate and what they will say, the reading loses its true healing potential. As I've explained many times in sessions, it's difficult for those on the other side to break through the density of someone's set beliefs or preconceived ideas. I often refer to this mental baggage as "agendas." It goes something like this:

Madelyn comes to a reading believing that if her deceased mother is actually communicating with her during the session, she will know and talk about the problems the family is having with settling her estate. That is the foremost issue on Madelyn's mind; nothing else really matters as far as she is concerned. After all, wouldn't her mom want her—not her unappreciative older sister—to get the valuable antique furniture? Further, since Madelyn was estranged from her deceased father for many years before he passed, he wouldn't possibly communicate anything to her in the session; even if he did, Madelyn wouldn't want to hear it. Imagine her surprise when, during the reading, her mother makes no mention of the estate and instead references fond memories of their mother-daughter relationship. Next, her dad steps in to say he's sorry for their estrangement. All of the incredible healing power of this information is crowded out by Madelyn's "agenda." She leaves the reading feeling one of two ways: I (the medium) am a fake or inept since I didn't meet her expectations and bring through what she wanted to hear, or her mother doesn't care about her since she didn't help solve the estate issue. Maybe both are true in her mind. In any event, her agenda seriously diluted the healing potential that her relatives in spirit were graciously offering. What can we learn from Madelyn's story? To get the most from a reading, it's always best to release personal expectations beforehand. What we believe is important is often not part of the BP, as those in spirit see it.

In all the years I've been doing readings, I've yet to have someone from the other side come through and express regret over not having worked longer hours, earned more money or owning more possessions in life. I doubt that will ever happen. In sharp contrast, I've read for clients who obsess over relatively insignificant details regarding money, real estate and other material possessions. The obvious fact is that when we return to spirit, we will take nothing physical with us. I believe those in spirit consider it their duty to remind us of this, since they often come through with what really matters in life—that is, nourishment for our souls. This is not to say that it is morally wrong to possess things, have money or admire beauty in the physical world. But since we do not truly own anything on earth (we only enjoy it for a limited time), we take only "what really matters" with us when we pass into spirit.

What *does* really matter according to those in spirit? The higher qualities of compassion, trust, forgiveness, service, healing, harmony, hope, peace, altruism, honesty and love feed and heal our souls and the planet. The BP is the lens through which the other side helps us to focus our hearts and minds on these qualities, which lead us to Spirit within. Most souls in spirit see precisely what really mattered to them, based on their choices, during their life review after passing. It is from this perspective that they communicate messages of healing and guidance for surviving family members.

Spirit guides and angels gently impress us with these higher qualities by connecting with us on a soul level, which is also called the Higher Self. This spark of the Divine in each of us is spiritually complete, always present and eternal. It is here that our guides and angels work with us through inspiration, intuition and healing to remember the perfection of who we are as embodiments of the Divine. They, however, cannot interfere with the karmic lessons that we have chosen to experience. Their role is to remind us of the existence of the higher qualities of our souls and how to embrace them.

The Role of Personal Responsibility in Spiritual Growth

Time and again, the other side has communicated in sessions that we are responsible for the quality and choices of our own lives. No one can do that for us. If we choose to disregard this higher guidance, we are free to do so. Those in spirit understand the concept of free will and our innate capacity to make our own choices, both good and bad. They help us grasp this truth so that we realize our power as spiritual beings and, in doing so, minimize needless suffering. I've stated this before but it bears repeating: those who didn't realize or embrace this truth while alive become aware of it during their life review after passing into spirit.

I've done many readings in which spirits come through and accept responsibility for their actions in life, especially if they didn't do so when they were alive. In some cases, they tell family members that something they did or didn't do was a direct factor in their death. For instance, I did a reading for a woman whose son was killed in a car accident while he was sending text messages on his cell phone. When he first came through, he impressed me with a strong sense that his actions caused his death. He went on to tell his mother that he neglected paying attention to her advice to not text and drive on many occasions. Then he referred to himself as stupid regarding his actions. His mother confirmed all of this and added that she loved and forgave him.

There is tremendous healing that occurs when people hear from deceased family members who "step up to the plate" and take responsibility for their actions. It's amazing that years of sadness, anger, regret and confusion can melt away in seconds. Forgiveness and transformation take place for everyone involved, (save for those who have a personal agenda), including family members from younger generations who never even knew the person in spirit. This example is an illustration:

Joseph, a businessman, experienced an emotionally charged session in which he heard from his deceased father, Robert, who had passed a decade earlier. Robert came through with messages about how he hadn't been a good father due to his over-concentration on work. Robert impressed me that he was a decent provider for his family, financially speaking, but that he had never validated his children with love—especially Joseph, the oldest son. He had imposed stringent expectations of performance and success on him. At one point during the session, Joseph's eyes filled with tears when his father said that he did indeed love him, even though he didn't communicate this when he was alive. Robert added that he wanted this unbalanced emotional pattern of emotional neglect to change with the younger generations—namely, Joseph's two sons, who were born after his passing. After the reading, Joseph shared that as a result of hearing from his dad, he wanted to re-evaluate his own life. He recognized that he had self-imposed perfectionism, which affected how he interacted with his sons. He had long wanted to become more emotionally connected to them and tell then he loved them. As a result of hearing from his father, Joseph vowed to change his priorities in life.

In some readings, spirits point out the value of "keeping one's slate clean"—or, to not create "negative" karma for oneself. Because we are responsible for our own thoughts, feelings and actions, we always take on the karmic repercussions from them.

Keeping our slate clean means to live in accordance with our Higher Self and not our ego, which, by its nature, interprets this "giving up" as a personal loss of power. We may also feel as if we've lost our self-respect in the process. Our soul perceives this from a much different perspective: disengaging from ego-centered thoughts and actions brings peace, harmony and preservation of the pure spiritual state of being.

Recently, I had the opportunity to sit with Amanda, whose grandchildren were not permitted to see her or the rest of the family—including her son, the children's father—by a spiteful, controlling ex-daughter-in-law, Judy. Amanda, emotionally distraught and bitter about the circumstances, wanted to know what she could do to change the way things were. Should she take Judy to court to force visitation? How could she do the best thing for her grandchildren? What if something horrible would happen to them- something she could have prevented? When Amanda's father (a wise, kind man) came through in the reading, he advised her to send prayers to not only the grandchildren but also Judy. He infused me with feelings of letting go, which I put into words for Amanda. He explained that what she needed to let go of was the need to control (coming from her own ego) the outcome of the situation. He advised that this was the choice that would keep Amanda's slate clean for now and that in the future, there would be a window of opportunity for healing in the family. He could see all of this from his perspective in spirit. I do not know which choice Amanda made but she left my office that evening with a much calmer demeanor than when she had arrived.

Keeping the slate clean means that despite the screams of our own ego to take retribution against others, we instead make choices that are in accordance with our Higher Self. We trust that the divine order of Spirit operates on our behalf, regardless of the appearance of outward circumstances. This path—the one of least resistance—ultimately serves the BP of our soul.

Divine Timing and Natural Order of Death

Sometimes, the BP delivered from the other side includes messages about why a certain death has occurred in the timeframe that it did. This is usually in response to people's questions about the seeming injustice of death; in other words, why do people (have to) die when they do? In sessions, souls in spirit have said that their lessons on earth were completed for the time being and they needed to return home. Although this rarely makes sense to us with our relatively narrow view of life, I believe it is nonetheless true. As is the case with our personal karma, we seldom fully comprehend why events transpire in the way and time they do. Acceptance and trust of divine order is needed to balance our doubt and confusion in these cases. When it is our time to cross over, we will see why life unfolded as it did.

I can think of no better reflection of the natural cycles of human birth, life and death than that found in nature. The only difference is that animals, trees, flowers, rocks and water do not have rational minds and personalities as we do. Yet they possess an innate intelligence that perpetually experiences change in the sustenance and evolution of life. In life, our ignorance of and resistance to this inherent rhythm causes us to needlessly suffer. The other side has revealed that if we look to the natural world as our teacher, we can greatly benefit in our understanding of death within the context of the divine flow and order of life. This is one of many ways in which communicating with souls in spirit has helped to transform my personal perceptions about life and death.

A reinforcement of the same truth came several years ago when I made a heart-wrenching decision to put down my dachshund, Emma, due to a debilitating lung condition. I'd spent five years pursuing every available treatment to improve the quality of her life; the endless array of pill bottles and breathing treatments that lined my kitchen shelves gave testament to that. Money was no object; I just wanted to save my dear Emma.

Despite all of this, when the day came to finally make the decision to stop treatment, I felt painfully guilty and desperately sad.

Before I left the veterinarian's office on that fateful day, the technician gave me a small pamphlet written by another veterinarian. One sentence stood out above the rest: our pets do not cling to life as we do. Although they have survival instincts, they are "wired" intuitively to know when it's time to die. It is we who strive (sometimes unreasonably and selfishly) to keep them alive because we cannot bear to let them go. The pamphlet went on to say that frequently our pets will stay with us beyond their natural time of death out of loyalty. This realization had a significant impact on what I had previously thought about human death, as well. Before then, I considered death as something that we, in our culture, take measures to delay and prevent at all costs. Isn't that good for us to do? Death is something to be avoided, isn't it?

Through my work as a medium, I know that grieving is undeniably painful to surviving family members and friends. But I also know- beyond any doubt- that we go on after leaving the physical world. After reading the pamphlet, I began to consider that death was a natural transition in life, one in which we (like our pets) don't actually die but return to the state of pure spirit. This realization felt right to me, intuitively speaking. Death shouldn't be demonized or feared, but recognized as a natural transition in the expression of the soul.

One day, I heard a startling answer from the other side that shed light on a commonly asked question regarding the suffering of loved ones during the dying process. Here's what happened:

At the start of our session, Rita announced that she had agonized for two years over what her late husband, Ron, had endured while dying from cancer. In the reading, Ron came through and stated that he compared dying to walking through a doorway into a building; that is, he went through a "portal" then released the process that had led him there. He impressed me with the thought of the number of doorways we typically step through in a day and how we don't give this a second thought; in other words, we do not lie awake at night and consciously recall or analyze these simple, everyday movements. Ron wanted me to tell Rita that he held no memory of the exit point to his new life. When I did so, immense relief washed over her worried face. She could now stop agonizing about how Ron died and move into acceptance of his continued existence in spirit. That reading has stuck with me and I have passed Ron's description along to others who are seeking comfort about the nature of passing into spirit.

Understanding death as a transition means that the soul is temporarily removing its focus from the physical plane and shifting it to the spirit world. Accepting that we will continue to exist in a different state of consciousness alleviates fear and eases the process of dying when that time comes.

Painful Experiences can be Used for Growth

I've had many experiences in which spirits come through and give reassurance to family members to move forward in life, despite distressing or tragic circumstances. In these cases, the BP they offer is especially influential in offering hope and encouragement during difficult times. This helps people navigate more easily through emotional recovery.

In a session I did for Diane, her daughter, Danielle, came through with a particularly powerful BP. Danielle was only 17 when she passed due to complications from a rare form of cancer. During the reading, Diane mentioned that one of the questions she had written before coming to the session was why Danielle had this debilitating illness. Spiritually speaking, why did she have to suffer? Listening to Danielle's response was eye opening and heartfelt for both of us. She impressed me that her illness and death were for the advancement of both her own spiritual growth and her family's. She filled me with feelings of gratitude for all of the people whose lives she had touched through her short time on earth (Danielle had been the subject of several newspaper articles and charity events.) Further, she showed me clairvoyant images of other teen-agers who would be helped by the research done on her case. The reading concluded with Danielle's exceptionally strong message of hope and gratitude for Diane's continued efforts in working with parents who had lost children to cancer.

The spiritually centered perspective that the BP offers is remarkable in that it instills in us an understanding of the divine order of life. Comprehending that we are all part of a universal intelligence that is innately harmonious and righteous, despite seeming inequities, gives new meaning to experiencing profound peace and trust in the process of life. This enables us to transcend the limitation of replaying the past and projecting ourselves into the unrealized future, which drains the vital energy needed to heal. We are then able to consolidate this energy into healing in present time.

Healing emotional pain means that we surrender resistance to what has happened and accept that in some way (even though we may not realize) it is an opportunity to awaken to our identity as spiritual beings. Resistance takes many forms—anger, guilt, sadness, depression and hopelessness—which all share the common thread of rejection (non-acceptance) of what has happened. To grow spiritually, it is necessary to first unconditionally accept painful conditions and circumstances of life as they are, in the present. By doing so, we enter into the spiritual state of our being, the place from which all healing emanates.

Many years ago in a 12-step recovery program, I learned about how holding resentments was counter-productive to recovery from substance abuse. Resentment means to feel negative feelings over and over again. It's as if we continually push a button that replays the past. The recovery program emphasizes that this is a sure-fire set-up to using substances again. Engaging in this type of thinking is clearly counterproductive to remaining clean. The suggested antidote for these spiritual toxins is to embrace forgiveness of the past, including forgiving ourselves. But first, we need to accept what we've done instead of covering it up with guilt, pity, a victim mentality and self-loathing. Then we can go about the business of releasing the past. This same process, when applied to healing emotional pain, gives us freedom from suffering undue anguish and remaining stagnant in spiritual growth.

In countless readings, souls in spirit have come through and urged loved ones that moving on in life is the best way to honor their memory. This clear-cut message helps to dissolve the mistaken belief that the amount of time people spend grieving for someone equals the depth of love they had for the deceased loved one. It is true that the painful experience of loss must be acknowledged and accepted; I am in no way recommending that it is right or healthy to not validate feelings. Rather, once feelings have been acknowledged, it is up to us to make the choice to see (with our spiritual eyes) beyond the pain. This is where spiritual growth begins.

I'm Here but My Body is There

On occasion, spirits talk about "viewing" their bodies shortly after death. The theme that is brought out in these communications is the continuation of the soul after shedding the shell of the body. Commonly, spirits make reference to what was going on just prior to or after dying. These messages contain compelling evidence of the soul's awareness after death. Consider this example concerning the sensation of floating upward and away from the body:

Tom sits with me as his late son, Brad, 18, comes through and describes his perspective after dying in a car accident.

"Dad, it was really cool," I relay to Tom. "I could see everything that was going on around me. I just kind of floated upward. It was awesome!"

I am infused with a feeling of wonder as I deliver the message. This boy makes dying seem like a sunny afternoon at an amusement park.

Tom chuckles softly and remarks, "That sounds just like Brad. He talked like that all the time. He was always curious about everything in life."

I continue with the communication. "Someone just said 'Mike.' Who is that?"

Tom's mouth drops open. "That's the man who found him right after the accident. He tried to save his life but it was too late. It's astounding that Brad knows about him. Now I *know* we are talking to Brad. Wow!"

Brad goes on to impress me that he stayed with his body until the ambulance soon came for it. He also references recent events within his family. His dad, although still in grief, leaves the session that day knowing his son's soul survived the accident.

Every so often, spirits make reference to attending their own funeral, including details about the service, people in attendance and what their body looks like. I believe that, for several reasons, most people attend their own funeral: Initially, there is sheer curiosity of being out of the body and viewing it objectively; attending the funeral helps to ease their way gradually out of physical existence and also gives an opportunity to be around those they knew and loved on earth. Additionally, in the case of spirits who didn't realize (due to a lack of spiritual consciousness) that they'll go on after physical life, being around the body after death helps them to awaken to this fact. Even so, these spirits may have to undergo counseling on the other side to make the necessary adjustment; the length of this adjustment period depends on the spiritual consciousness of souls and how open they are to receiving help on the other side.

In that light, I've seen how souls who have taken their own

life through suicide are often surprised to realize that they are still "alive" after they die physically. Several years ago, my friend, Alice, and I attended the funeral of 25-year-old Jason, who had taken his own life. Alice has been clairvoyant most of her life, although she doesn't work as a medium. Before I left the viewing room that day, I turned to shake the hand of Jason's mother. Out of the corner of my eye, I saw Jason as he had appeared in life standing on the left side of the casket and looking down at his body. I was startled yet not really surprised to see him there. As we walked to the parking lot after the viewing, I asked Alice if she had noticed Jason in spirit. She answered that she had perceived him in the exact same place that I had — on the left side of the casket, peering curiously at his body.

In readings, spirits sometimes give messages about how relieved they are to be out of their physical body. I once did a reading for Kim, whose late brother, Bob had ALS, a debilitating illness that ultimately paralyzes the body's muscles. She had been Bob's primary caretaker. When Bob came through, he impressed me that he had felt like a prisoner in his body, since the disease had made him an invalid. Bob expressed that he felt elation in having shed the body that had encumbered him in his last years of life. He showed me that he was now dancing in his spirit body — an activity that he had enjoyed before he became ill. He also impressed me that this image of himself was symbolic of his freedom of movement in his new spirit body. When I relayed all of this to Kim, she cried and said that she found comfort in knowing that her brother was finally at peace after a long, difficult struggle.

The Bonds and Rewards of Love Continue Forever

If there is one thing that I hope to communicate in this book, it is that the love we share with our families, friends and pets survives forever. Because we are Spirit at our core, we come into physical existence from that eternal, inexhaustible source and we return to it when physical life ends. Through many years of communicating with the other side, I've learned that the inescapable, undeniable truth is that we will take only love (in whatever form it was expressed) with us when we return to our true home. While we are here, we will encounter situations that challenge us to draw on the strength of that love, which is ours by birthright. Maybe the boiled-down version of the BP that those on the other side have to offer is this: *nothing can ever diminish, surpass or destroy the all-encompassing love of Spirit within each individual.* This is who we have always been, are now and will be beyond death. When we really *get* this truth and know it to be so, we spiritually awaken. In that moment we are free.

Three

Beyond the Physical Realm

Life and death are one, even as the river and the sea are one.
In the depths of your hopes and desires lies your silent knowledge of
the beyond;
and like seeds dreaming beneath the snow, your heart dreams of
spring.
Trust the dreams, for in them is hidden the gate to eternity.
Kahlil Gabran

As we travel on our earthly journey in the physical world, we
often forget that we are inextricably connected to our home in the
spirit world. You have no doubt heard the expression that we are
spiritual beings who are having human experiences. But if that is
the case, why do we so often struggle against or deny this fundamental truth? How does our physical existence become so intox-
icating that we lose touch with who we really are? At times, we
become overly identified with our earthly lives and forget our
spiritual identity—until we experience wake-up calls that alert us
to our true nature. When we, as immortal souls, incarnate into the
finite physical world, we are subject to its conditions of duality,
contrast and the illusion of separation from the higher worlds of
Spirit. When our expansive, eternal souls take limited form in a
dense physical body, we have agreed (in our blueprints) to
experience certain circumstances on earth that will help us to
remember our real spiritual identity. During that journey, we
remain connected to, not separate from, other spiritual realms.

Understanding that we are never separate from other realms
means that we recognize ourselves as spiritual beings who are
indeed having human experiences in order to evolve. In this

chapter, you will see how the physical world interconnects with the spirit world (also called the astral plane), what it's like there and the relationship between the two.

A frustrating barrier I've attempted to hurdle in writing about spiritual realms is the English language, which has few words that convey succinct definitions of nonphysical reality. Terms such as "energy" and "vibration" can be limiting and repetitive, yet I know of no others that would better apply. My hope is that I've chosen the best words to help you understand what the spirit world is like and what souls there experience in terms of spiritual consciousness.

Before we explore the other side and its connection to us, it's necessary to understand exactly what I mean when I refer to the spirit world. There are many realms of consciousness besides the physical one, of which the spirit or astral plane is but one. "Plane" refers to a level of consciousness. The higher the level is from the physical one, the purer the spiritual consciousness one would find present there. Likewise, the further one goes beyond the physical level, the higher the vibration of that plane. For our purposes here (unless I note otherwise), when I refer to the spirit world, I mean the level of consciousness where most "average" souls go upon passing from the physical world. The higher worlds- those above the astral realm- are home to spiritually enlightened beings, such as the ascended masters (Jesus, Buddha and Krishna)) and the saints (St. Germain, St. Francis, St. Theresa and many others.) The angelic realm also exists in the higher worlds of Spirit. As our spiritual consciousness ascends from lifetime to lifetime, we will naturally be drawn to that corresponding level in the spirit world upon death. If you are interested in learning about higher levels of spiritual consciousness than the astral realm, I suggest you read esoteric philosophy books, like those of the early theosophists such as Alice Bailey or Madame Blavatsky.

The topics I am writing about in this chapter are the ones

that I've encountered frequently in my work and through my metaphysical studies. I addressed them below in the form of questions that people frequently come to my sessions with. I've chosen ones that I feel will give you the best understanding of the other side, our continued relationship with loved ones who are there and the interwoven connection between the two worlds.

Where is the spirit world?

Over the years, I've been asked where the spirit world is located, physically speaking. The truth is that since it is not a place but rather a state of consciousness, the issue of location is not relevant. It is right here, surrounding us, wherever we happen to be. We are not normally aware of it since most people's consciousness is primarily concerned with awareness of the physical world. Perceiving the relatively subtle realm of the spirit world is a matter of tuning into it through the inner senses, much like tuning a radio to a particular frequency.

As I described in Chapter One, I tune into this awareness when I do readings. Radio and TV signals are constantly being broadcast, but if we do not have the radio or TV on, we will not pick up the signals. Although not everyone has the sensitivity of a medium, each of us has access to the inner senses that operate from the soul level of awareness. Development of the three main inner senses (clairvoyance, clairaudience and clairsentience) through meditation and repeated use increases one's sensitivity to the spirit world. One sense may be more strongly expressed than the other two, depending on how much spiritual consciousness and development has taken place. The point is that the frequency of the spirit world is not detected through the five physical senses and is not limited to place or time.

You may be familiar with the expression, "as above, so below," which refers to the relationship between heaven and earth. To understand this, consider that the relationship between the physical world and the spirit realm can be compared to looking into a mirror; that is, everything that exists in the physical world has a counterpart on the other side. The notable difference is that everything in the spirit world is amorphous, fluid-like and flowing, compared to the finite, dense forms that occupy the physical world. To simplify even further, think of the physical world as comprised of stone and the spirit world of water. Souls who exist in spirit are in a realm where thought and not physicality, predominates.

The mirror comparison also refers to the fact that thought precedes the manifestation of form or matter. This means that everything in the physical world was first a thought or idea, a feeling or a combination of the two. The amount of focus and desire (the intensity of feeling and personal will) applied to thought determines how quickly the thought will manifest into physical form. In the spirit world, souls can generate thoughts and instantly manifest them on the astral level. For example, they can think about a place on earth and immediately be at that location in their consciousness. Travel is instantaneous. This is how loved ones can be around us all the time. They merely need to think of us and they are here with us. The physical impediments of "distance" and "time" do not apply. To further grasp this concept, consider that it takes only an instant to think a thought; that is how quickly souls in spirit can move about.

Where do we go after death?

Just as there are many levels of consciousness above the physical one, the astral world itself contains many levels, each varying in the quality of the vibration of energy present within it. Put simply, the higher levels resonate more purely with the divine force than the lower ones. In the higher levels, there is awareness of the unity of all of creation, with no illusion of duality or separation. Spirit is perceived and recognized as the underlying, cohesive energy uniting all souls and the entire universe. Using the physical level as a base point, each successive level increases in vibration and purity of spiritual consciousness the further away one moves from the physical plane. Most souls (ordinary people who have led decent lives) go to the mid-levels upon passing. The lower levels (those closest to the earth) are where earthbound spirits (those who are unable to let go of their earthly attachments) and souls who had little to no spiritual awareness go after passing. If these souls are willing, they can receive counseling from specially trained helping spirits to move beyond their former consciousness. Love and compassion are the healing balms that help these souls move on to the higher levels of the astral plane.

The life we lead on earth determines our placement in the spirit world following death. If we were "good" people who led a relatively harmonious and service-oriented life, we will go to a place that matches that level of spiritual consciousness. On the other hand, if we were selfish, hurt others or committed crimes, we will find ourselves in the lower levels of the spirit world with other souls who also lived as we did. This is because we alone are always responsible for our own soul and not at the mercy of an outside punishing force. The universal law of karma, which operates within each person, is the divine system of justice that ensures we receive in life what we give to ourselves, others and the world. If we were not aware of this truth during life, we will certainly know it at the time of death, when a life review takes place within our consciousness. We are then shown the implications of the choices we made in life, how our actions and words affected others and the overall quality of our life. From this point, we are naturally drawn to the corresponding level in the astral world that matches the consciousness we left earth with. Our new life in spirit has begun!

Is my loved one okay? How can I be sure?

One of the most common questions I'm asked is whether deceased loved ones are "okay" in spirit. Because I am an

Beyond the Physical Realm

evidential medium—one who provides facts about the identity and continued existence of souls in spirit—I feel it is my responsibility to give more than a simple "yes" or "no" answer. So instead of doing that, I ask spirit beings to impress me with some type of message that indicates their interconnectedness with living family members. This typically involves their making reference to recent events and circumstances in the lives of their loved ones. Since many people seek reassurance that they are still connected with souls they knew and loved in life, these types of messages are particularly comforting. At times, the messages are uncannily specific, thus giving concrete validation that loved ones are aware of their family's lives. The other side uses such messages as proof that they are alive in spirit and aware of life in the physical realm. The next example is taken from a recent session:

During Betty's reading, her only daughter, Karen, came through and gave evidence of how she died from a blood clot after surgery. The reading continued with Karen validating her identity by giving her name and other specifics. The communication then turned to recent evidence that Karen had given her mother to let her know she was around. In my mind, a clairvoyant image of a clock on a stove suddenly appeared. When I shared this with Betty, her face instantly lit up in recognition. I went on to say that Karen impressed me that she had come around her mother when she was in the kitchen.

"Yes! " Betty exclaimed. "I've felt her there, near my stove. But there is something that has happened lately to that clock that I've wondered about. What I mean is, I thought she was doing something to it. Can she tell me if she is?"

I went into my zone to listen to Karen's answer. She made me feel that she was definitely involved with the clock incident and that she clearly wanted her mother to know that. Further, she showed me that she had made the clock flicker or change in some way. I passed this information along to Betty and her eyes again

59

lit up.

"Twice I've seen my digital clock stove flash the numbers of my birth date," she said excitedly. "I have no explanation for how or why this happened. I knew it was her doing that!"

"She is sending you signals to let you know she was okay," I added.

Betty left the session that day beaming because she knew her daughter was undoubtedly with her through the validation of the clock incident.

Souls in spirit want us to know that they are with us and they go on in other levels of consciousness. They do not want us to stop living our lives or mourn their passing to the point of neglecting our own happiness. In fact, in many readings, they come through and urge family members to move on in life and not worry about them. At times, they express concern over living family members' lives far more than talking about themselves. Although this may seem odd, I believe it is because their point of view (the BP) affords them the spiritual perspective of the divine order of life and death, which they attempt to communicate during sessions. So, in the true sense of the word, they are assuredly "okay."

Do they miss me? How do I get over missing them?

It is from the same vantage point—the BP—that those in spirit view their relationships with us. Upon death, we become aware of the interconnectedness of our soul with all others and with life as a whole. It is from this perspective that "missing" someone becomes non-relevant, since all souls are connected and being with others is a spiritual matter, not a physical one. When we die, we become aware of this fundamental spiritual truth. As I mentioned earlier, those on the other side can be with us as quickly as a thought. It is our limited perspective in the physical realm that perceives the illusion of separation. In fact, we can actually be closer to those in spirit, since distance and physicality no longer apply.

On the flip side of this spiritual reality is our human perception of loss. After years of doing readings, I've learned that most people must go through a grieving process that necessitates mourning the physical presence of loved ones. We cannot deny that someone is no longer with us in a physical sense and that loss causes us pain. Touching or talking with someone in a physical sense cannot be replaced by or compared to sharing a spiritual relationship with him. Our physical bodies are palpable and real to us. To move beyond the pain, we must first acknowledge what we feel and let grieving take place. Allowing these feelings to surface and expressing them openly makes coping with loss an easier process. Moving beyond grief means not getting stuck in feelings that no longer serve the continued expression of our soul. Such thoughts deny the immortality of the soul. We must recognize that physical reality is only one aspect of a relationship and that the spiritual connection we share need not be diminished by death.

Some people never get over losing or missing loved ones. In my experience, this is especially true when parents lose children, no matter the age. In all the years I've done readings, I have yet to meet a parent who has not been deeply and irreversibly transformed by their loss. Yet, when these children have come through in sessions, they communicate that they give encouragement to their parents to continue on in life despite their seemingly untimely passing. I've also seen how grieving parents move beyond grief and suffering by honoring their deceased children's lives by living their own lives as best they can after experiencing such a catastrophic event. Living life means developing and maintaining spiritual awareness day by day, moment by moment. People in grief who stay connected to a spiritual presence have an easier time of moving through loss. By doing so, they offer hope and service to others who are likewise struggling with loss.

Many years ago, I learned in 12-step recovery that the best way to "get out of my own way" and develop the core spiritual connection to maintain sobriety was to reach out and help others. In my circumstance, this meant that I needed to be present for and help others who were not as far along as I was in recovery. On a practical level this meant giving a ride to someone in need, cleaning up after meetings, volunteering to speak at 12-step groups and being a friend to someone who was lonely. Overcoming the huge mountain of self-pity that I dwelled in daily was no easy feat but once I finally got rolling, life greatly improved. My spiritual awareness and healing increased in direct proportion to the release of my self-centeredness. This recognition of the light of Spirit within me—previously concealed by years of substance abuse—led me to reach out to others more, which at the same time, helped me.

I believe the same philosophy of 12-step recovery can be applied to healing any issue in life, including the loss of loved ones. Although there are no guarantees we'll get over missing someone, it *is* possible to reach out of our own darkness and be present for others, regardless of circumstances. In that moment, we have taken the opportunity to awaken to the spiritual presence, the divine healing force within ourselves and others.

What do we do on the other side?

Kelly, whose 22-year-old son, Trevor, had passed, was curious about what he had been "doing" on the other side. At the beginning of our session, Kelly asked if I could help her find answers to come to peace with her son's death. After bringing through evidence of his continued existence in spirit, I saw Trevor in my mind's eye standing in front of a group of young spirits in a schoolroom-like setting. The feeling that accompanied this image was that Trevor was mentoring others in spirit. When I described this image to Kelly, she responded with excitement that the image made sense to her, since Trevor had graduated from college with a teaching degree a few months before he died in a car accident. He loved to be around children and had planned to use his training to help them. Obviously, Trevor was carrying on with the work he had begun in his physical life.

Through years of working as a medium and studying metaphysics, I've discovered that most souls carry on with the work they were doing on earth. The well-known vision of souls communing with angels sitting on fluffy clouds does not apply to most of us. Maybe there are exceptions but I am not personally acquainted with them. What *does* happen after death is the continued growth of our souls. Not only do we take our spiritual consciousness with us when we cross over, we take our earthly pastimes and pursuits, as well. In readings, I have seen spirits who are engaged in activities (reading, fishing or gardening, for example) that they did on earth.

The same applies to carrying on with work and study in the spirit world. I once did a reading in which a woman wanted to know what her late boyfriend was doing since he passed. At the very moment she asked the question, an image of a large stack of books appeared in my mind. Further, her boyfriend impressed me that he had enjoyed being a lifelong student while alive. She validated these messages and added that she was at peace knowing that he was doing what made him happy.

Of course, the very nature of the spirit world makes "doing" impossible—at least in the physical sense as we know it. Perhaps it is more accurate to say that souls *think* about doing something and are then instantly doing it. "Being" is a state that exists in the astral world—an existence without past or future. We can access this same timeless, expansive state by practicing meditation, which also opens the door to sensing the spirit world with greater clarity. It is from this consciousness that we realize there is no beginning, end or interruption to our soul's existence, despite our perceived illusion of it. There is only continuity of Spirit.

What does age at death have to do with the soul's age on the other side?

The age of the soul has little to do with the age we are when we make transition to the spirit world or our current age, for that matter. For instance, I've done readings for sitters in their 20's who were relatively old souls who had lived many lifetimes on earth. On the other hand, I've connected with people in spirit who, despite being very old at the time of death, were relatively young souls.

When children come through in readings, I sense them as the age they were when they passed (this is also an easy way for family members to identify them). I've done readings in which infants come through and use the same evidence as spirits who were adults when they passed. For example, I once read for a woman over the phone whose six-month-old daughter in spirit came through with details of what items had been placed in her casket, her favorite toys and who she was with in the spirit world. The child's mother cried with both sorrow and joy at hearing from her baby. I sensed an enormous amount of light emanating from this baby's soul, who was clearly an advanced soul who had come to earth to help her family with specific spiritual lessons. Her grieving mother expressed gratitude when I shared this information with her at the conclusion of the reading.

People who are overwhelmed by the deaths of loved ones relatively early in life want to know why someone's life would be cut short, especially when the future seemed so bright. I do not believe there is a simple answer that can be applied to all cases of younger passings. In my work, I've seen how souls have agreed to come into life to balance karmic connections with family members, advance humanitarian causes and master specific spiritual qualities. Any or all of these can be true, depending on the unique consciousness of souls. Perhaps the most important thing to remember in these cases is to trust in the innate goodness, harmony and justice of Spirit. As mentioned earlier, our soul's spiritual mission is seldom crystal clear when we are in physical reality. Accepting that this will be revealed to us upon passing is helpful and comforting.

Since the soul is eternal, it is not concerned with or limited by time or age. Its true awareness knows only unity, perfection and unconditional love. It does not care whether it takes five or 500 incarnations to learn the spiritual quality of compassion, for example. Its sole intent is to express itself infinitely and eternally. When we return to our true home, we become aware of the magnitude and beauty of who we really are—despite age, gender, race or any other physical condition. (In Chapter Seven, I will further discuss the lack of peace with loved ones' deaths and how to find solace.)

What do dreams tell us about the other side and loved ones in spirit?

Most clients report having dreams in which deceased loved ones appear. Although there is no single theme to these dreams, what they share is the connection of those in spirit with souls here on earth. Not every dream is a true visitation with the other side; some are concerned with working out emotional and psychological issues within the dreamer. Actual visitations from loved ones will feel compellingly, startlingly real; that is, we know beyond all doubt that we are with that soul in a timeless moment. When people ask me to verify that their visitation with a loved one is real, I ask them one question: *Did it feel incredibly real in the sense that the person was there with you?* If so, chances are it was a visitation; if not, the dream is probably their way of working through their own human thoughts and emotions.

The other factor to consider in dream visitations is that those in spirit will visit us when *they* want and not when we request it. Over the years, I've talked with many people who want to have a dream visitation so desperately that they become unhealthily attached to the idea. When it doesn't happen (especially in their timing), they feel cheated, angry and hopeless. I've also encountered people who are jealous because other family members or friends have received visitations and they have not. Unfortunately, we cannot wave a magic wand and force those in spirit to communicate with us on our time schedule. I wish it were that easy but this is not the way it works in dreams or mediumship. Ironically, letting go of the need to experience a visitation is the best thing to do. This may allow it to happen but there are no guarantees. Being receptive and gently inviting those in spirit to come through if they want is helpful.

In *I'm Still With You*, I described a dream visitation that I had with my father's mother that I will never forget. In it, she appeared exactly as I remembered her, even though she had passed many years prior. The most memorable quality of that dream was the pure love that I felt flowing between us. No words were exchanged. Years later, I still experience the emotional potency of that brief encounter when I think about it.

Why would loved ones choose to come to us in dreams? It's easier for those in spirit (including spirit guides and teachers) to reach us when we are in receptive states such as sleep and meditation—when our rational, analytical brain is not in control. Beyond that, loved ones come through to communicate their continued connection with us and to impart messages of love and guidance. When we are sleeping, our astral consciousness temporarily separates from our physical body. During that time, we visit the astral plane and higher levels of Spirit to "recharge our spiritual batteries." When it is time to wake, our astral consciousness reconnects with our physical body. When we are sleeping, we also have clearer access to the unconscious or universal mind, which consists of everything, everywhere- past, present and future.

Because this book addresses healing soul connections between people, I'd like to mention that in dreams, loved ones can come through and offer forgiveness and encouragement for living family members. An example of this from my case files is a husband who visited his wife one night and told her that he was sorry for the argument they'd had just prior to his passing. The woman had felt emotionally tortured for a year by this final exchange, which was angry and bitter. After the dream visitation, she was finally able to move on in the grieving process. In other cases, when loved ones simply appear in a dream without direct communication, the message is usually something like, "I'm fine and doing well in my new home. Please don't worry about me. Go on with your life."

Another type of dream involves the dreamer encountering loved ones on the other side then being told it is not yet their time to cross into the spirit world. Often, some sort of physical boundary is shown in the dream that communicates the idea that the timing is not right for the dreamer to cross over. This happened to Justine, whose son Greg was in spirit. One night she had a dream in which Greg appeared and clearly told her to stop thinking about coming to be with him, since it wasn't her time to do so. He appeared to Justine behind a thick, glass wall. Before he left, he told his mother they would be with one another again when it was her proper time to pass. In our session, Justine admitted she had thought many times about taking her own life because of her immense grief over losing Greg. The dream changed her entire emotional state from one of despair to hope that she would one day be with her son again.

Have you had visitations in which a deceased loved one communicated information about you or your loved one's lives? Many people have. These dreams are their way of continuing to help us with our earthly journey. In these encounters, we may hear of events yet to unfold in our lives, such as the birth of a baby, healing from an illness or relocating to another state.

Not all dreams are pleasant ones. At some time or another, we have all had a dream that centered on a painful, unresolved emotional issue. One young woman I met with described a dream in which she saw her late mother in extreme physical pain suffering from cancer, which had claimed her life several years earlier. In it, she could not reach out to her mother due to a large wall that appeared between them. She asked me what I thought the dream meant and whether her mom was trying to tell her something. I told her my sense was that it was not a visitation but rather her own subconscious working out the emotions of helplessness surrounding her mom's death. She validated this when she admitted that she had felt powerless to control her mother's death and that she wished she'd had done more for her. She had felt that she couldn't save her from the disease that was ravaging her body. The dream was her way of getting in touch with her own feelings of powerlessness and guilt.

In some instances, loved ones come through in dreams and tell family members of an impending death. Although disturbing, I believe they want to help us to be emotionally prepared for death when it happens. Although it's difficult to do, if you should have a dream such as this, don't let it control your thoughts. Simply accept it, knowing that if you are meant to act in some way that could change the outcome of the dream, that you will intuitively be given what is needed.

I've spoken with people who have had vivid dreams about what the other side looks like, what they did while there and who they saw. Because we regularly disconnect with our physical bodies during sleep, we frequently travel to the astral realm for purposes of study, to cleanse our emotional bodies and to receive spiritual healing. As described earlier, it is a natural process for the thread of our astral consciousness to temporarily withdraw from our waking consciousness and to reconnect with the spirit world. Out-of-body experiences are the same process but happen when people are awake.

The spirit world has several striking qualities that come through in dreams: vivid colors, fluid surroundings and the instant manifestation and animation of the dreamer's thoughts and feelings. Sensations of floating, drifting and flying are also common. People may find themselves engaged in activities that they do in life but with an expanded or elevated vision of that activity. We can also meet with others who are living in the physical world if we so choose.

I once had a dream in which I found myself doing hands-on healing in a hospital-like setting on the other side. At that time in my life, I volunteered at doing Reiki (a form of hands-on healing) at an HIV outreach program in my community. In the dream, I was doing healing for a man I had met at the center several weeks earlier. When I awoke, I felt an incredible sense of peace, compassion and satisfaction that I had helped someone in need. The dream gave me a deeper perspective of my training as a healer and how it was touching others' lives.

How do loved ones let us know they're around us?

Through my work, I've connected with hundreds of people who have received spirit communication without the assistance of a medium. Many of these circumstances appear to be authentic communication from the other side, although not all have been validated as such. In most, there is no logical, rational explanation for how the phenomena are produced through known physical laws. Interestingly, these signs from the non-physical world often manifest to people through physical reality. This is another example of how we are not separate from the higher worlds of Spirit and how our earthly consciousness is interconnected with the spiritual realms.

Some of the common signs that people have reported receiving from the other side are telephone calls (with no one on the other end) from one's own number; electrical devices such as lights that flash or TV sets that spontaneously turn off and on; strange smells with no physical origin; coins appearing in unexpected places; objects that are moved in the home or office; birds and other animals that congregate around the home or porch; numbers and initials related to the deceased that repeatedly come up; and imprinted audio recordings (electronic voice phenomena, or EVP) that are unexplainable. I do not know how these phenomena are produced but it is obviously some sort of merging of spiritual energy with the physical plane, and further demonstration of the unity of the material world with higher dimensions. Souls who achieve this must lower their vibration to do so, since the spirit world vibrates at a higher velocity than earth. I believe this is accomplished through the focused concentration of their thoughts.

In some cases, signs are produced on the anniversary of a loved one's passing into spirit or a significant date such as a birthday or wedding anniversary. This type of communication gives reassurance and comfort to those who receive it. The flip side of this is when people become dismayed when the signs suddenly cease or are not produced at all. If this has happened to you, the important thing to consider is that these signs are gifts from those in spirit and, as such, should not have expectations attached to them—just as it's not the right sentiment to "expect" a gift from other loved ones in your life. The less we become dependant on needing physical signs from the other side, the more we can open to a spiritual connection with loved ones, a bond that lasts forever.

Another way that those on the other side communicate with us is through producing physical sensations in our bodies. I've done many readings in which the communicating spirit impresses me that they have "touched" living family members around the head, neck or shoulder area, given them a hug or created a tingling feeling in some part of the body. The key to knowing if these sensations are spiritually produced is to go within oneself to discern whether any feelings or images accompany the sensations. For example, my mother in spirit has come to me at night when I am lying in bed meditating by creating a tingling sensation in my legs. When this initially happened several years ago, I not only saw her in my mind's eye, I heard her (through clairaudience) as she offered words of encouragement to me about a troubling personal situation. Mom's presence was pleasant and comforting. She doesn't come to me in this way all the time, so I really cherish these visits when they happen.

When we are in the process of dying, do others in spirit come to help us cross over?

If you've ever sat with a dying person, you may have seen or heard them reach out and talk to deceased family members and friends who have come to help during the transition. In observing this, we can only imagine the joyous reunion that takes place between souls who may have been physically separated for years. In the case of sudden or unanticipated deaths, deceased family members are aware on a soul level of the passing and will come to lend help. Many spirits who have connected with me during readings convey that they were present during the deaths of recently departed loved ones. Often, they will identify themselves by name or their physical condition when they passed. In my experience, deceased family members and friends assist not only before and during the death process but afterwards in what I call the "acclimation" or "adjustment" stage. During this time, the personality and earthly consciousness are shed because they are no longer needed. The newly departed spirit must adapt to moving around without the physical body, recall the power and strength of his spiritual consciousness and continue his existence on the other side.

To give you a better idea how spirits have come through in my client readings to validate their presence during the dying process, I've come up with the following sketch, which is a composite from hundreds of readings I've done.

Corey wanted to know if her dad (deceased a decade before her mom) came for her mom when she passed. Corey was very concerned that her mom (a timid, emotionally dependent woman) had not been able to find her way on the other side. When I tuned in, her mom told me that not only had her late husband come for her, so did an older female with a name that begins with the letters A-N. Corey immediately recognized that she was referring to her maternal grandmother, Anna. The mother went on to tell Corey that she was with her father (Corey's grandfather), who long ago passed from cancer, as well as her uncle, who had worked as a carpenter. Corey understood all of this. Her mom offered clear and irrefutable evidence that validated who helped her cross over at the time of death which gave her daughter much needed peace.

Spirit guides are also available to help souls cross over at the time of death. These loving beings assist in the transition process by compassionately guiding the newly departed spirit back home to the appropriate place in the astral plane. Once there, guides help in the life review that souls experience by giving insight and support about important life lessons. They also watch over and give guidance about the adjustments new spirits must make once they leave their physical bodies.

What about departed souls who remain attached to the earth plane? Are they what people refer to as "ghosts"?

It is true that there are souls who choose to remain attached to levels of the astral plane that are the densest and closest to earth. As such, these levels are relatively dark in terms of the amount of spiritual light that is generated there and lower in vibration than higher levels of the astral plane. The higher levels emanate more light because their vibration is more closely aligned to the unity of the Divine than the duality found on earth. The souls that reside in the levels closest to earth are not necessarily bad or evil; they have simply chosen to remain attached to their former earthly consciousness instead of shedding it, as most spirits do after passing.

There are several reasons why spirits remain attached to these lower astral levels. In some cases, the attachment is primarily emotional; the spirit cannot let go of his earthly home for one reason or another. In some cases, the emotional attachment may be the result of a tragic event that happened to either the soul or other family members, such as the death of a child, a devastating fire, an accident or suicide. This doesn't mean that experiencing any of these circumstances automatically implies that souls will remain in the lower astral regions; rather, the determining factor in how expediently a soul "moves on" at the time of death is the spiritual consciousness of that soul and therefore, how its life circumstances are emotionally received, processed and resolved.

The inability to let go of painful or tragic life events by maintaining a strong emotional connection to them keeps spirits on the lower levels, even when they are not what we would call "ghosts", that is, scary apparitions who haunt buildings. In other words, unfinished emotional attachments to earthly life must be released before entering into a higher level of consciousness in the spirit world.

The closer a spirit remains to earth in terms of its spiritual vibration, the stronger its desires and emotions. This is because the attachment to the physical plane is created through emotion and desire—states of consciousness that create karma that subsequently must be balanced. That is why physical locations where strong emotions have been expressed (fear, anger, panic, hatred, sadness or jealousy) are more likely to house lower astral souls. Examples are prisons, mental health institutions, some bars and pubs, battlefields and any place in which strong emotions have been imprinted on the environment. I've talked with people who have reported encountering earthbound spirits in these types of locations. I have long felt, based on what I've observed that these emotionally charged atmospheres contain energy imprints from their former living inhabitants and the events that transpired there. The scientific investigations into these types of "hauntings" have revealed that there are verifiable, active intelligences present in these locations. Whether they are actual souls or energy imprints in the atmosphere that replay over time (like a recording) continues to be investigated by many paranormal researchers.

Sometimes, the emotions held by spirits can be positive ones, such as extreme devotion or loyalty—which was the case in a spiritual facility I once attended. The building, a former Catholic grade school, was constructed in the early 20th Century. Every so often, members of the spiritual group that met in this building saw apparitions and felt the presence of nuns in the chapel area. When I've attended services there, my sense has been that these spirits consider themselves to be guardians of this peaceful place.

Several years ago, I led a psychic investigation of a pet spa, where the owner and employees reported seeing apparitions of Native Americans throughout the building and surrounding property. During the investigation, I sensed many spirits in and around the building, including a child by an indoor pool and a beautiful young Native American woman who seemed to be intrigued with the center's modern washer and dryer where employees spotted her on several occasions. The owner also reported electrical malfunctions throughout the building. At the end of my visit, I asked two employees to take photos of the land surrounding the building. Within minutes, we viewed numerous glowing orbs (signs of spirit presence) in the photos. I sensed that these earthbound spirits meant no harm and were merely acting as guardians of the land, which was later revealed through research to have been their home many, many years ago. The facility was situated squarely on the energy vortex of this "charged" land, which accounted for the strange manifestations in the building.

In some cases, addiction to substances such as alcohol, drugs or tobacco can keep spirits (those who were unable to let go of these while alive) earthbound because they vicariously experience the effects of these substances through those who are using them on the earth plane. These substances weaken the aura (the energy field) of users, causing it to be vulnerable and open to outside energetic influences, such as lower astral entities. This doesn't mean that earthbound spirits "possess" users who are in the body; rather, they hover around their energy fields in order to get high or feel a buzz. This is just one of many reasons to avoid addictive substances.

If you do not use substances, but are sensitive to energy, you may have visited certain bars or pubs where you felt unpleasant feelings of agitation, sadness or general unease. In these cases, it's advisable to leave as soon as possible. If that's not an option, I recommend putting on energetic "armor" to protect yourself. You can envision a bright violet flame (which dissolves lower energies) around your entire auric field and call on your Higher Self to protect you from outside influences.

Helping earthbound spirits move on into the spirit world should be undertaken by someone with expertise in doing this type of work. To find someone in your area, ask for references from friends or reputable mediums, or check listings related to paranormal investigations on the Internet.

Do pets come back to visit after they pass?

The answer to this is a resounding "yes." In thousands of readings I've done, pets have come through with clients' deceased family members and friends. Because they are Spirit, just as we are, they do not die when they leave the physical plane. I've seen them on the other side in beautiful, outdoor settings such as vibrant, green meadows and lush fields. Like humans, if they were ill or decrepit before passing, they enjoy the true freedom of being in their spirit bodies.

Frequently, I've talked with people who relate stories of feeling, hearing or smelling a deceased pet. One woman told me about seeing her late dog in his favorite spot in the kitchen, near his treat jar. Another shared an incident in which she awoke one morning sensing her late 16-year-old cat in bed, curled around her neck, just as he had always done. Several years ago when I was alone in my house, I heard my late dachshund, Emma, bark. I've also seen her clairvoyantly in various places throughout the house.

I believe pets come to us as healers, entering our lives when their presence is required then exiting when their work is complete. Although we may not fully understand the reasons at the time, they connect with us spiritually and touch us in ways that our conscious mind cannot fathom. Our relationships with them can be just as vital, inspiring and conducive to our spiritual growth as the ones we share with humans.

If we accept that we are undeniably connected to the higher worlds of Spirit, we realize that we are not and never have been separate from those who have crossed over. By virtue of the strength of that love within us, we are capable of letting go of grief and healing unfinished emotional business that weighs us down. The only requirement is that we open our hearts to allow the all-encompassing love of Spirit to flow through us, unrestrained by our own fear. In that illuminating light, we will know peace.

PART TWO:

SOUL CONNECTIONS

Four

How Could This Happen?

Earth has no sorrow that heaven cannot heal.
St. Thomas More

The pathway of spiritual growth reveals that self-knowledge is both our journey and our destination. Of all the lessons that life presents to us, the ones that are often the most compelling, poignant and memorable are those that touch our souls through emotion. Whether these experiences positively or negatively impact us, they are imprinted on our souls. Not coincidentally, these lessons are also the ones that frequently test the strength of our love for another, transform our long-held beliefs or challenge the very core of our identity through crisis.

As souls who have come to earth to evolve in a physical setting, we must learn to overcome self-defeating emotional patterns that keep us tethered to levels of fear that severely limit us in so many ways. If we learn to view emotions as indicators of our spiritual consciousness, we can use them as wake-up calls that point us toward greater alignment with Spirit. If we choose to ignore the call, we are destined to experience similar lessons until we gain mastery over our own ego. In the end, each of us must face our own life review and be accountable for the life we have chosen to live. We will clearly see every opportunity we have been given to validate either light or darkness within ourselves.

Each time we are presented with life circumstances that are beyond our conscious understanding, we make a choice to respond either with fear (generated through our ego) or with faith in the divine order of Spirit. In the course of a day, we have numerous opportunities to subjugate our precious life force to the demands of ego, or grace it with the awareness of Spirit. The separating, fear-based emotions of anger, blame, resentment, guilt, selfishness and shame cast shadows over our hearts, which are innately designed to give and accept love. On an energy scale of one to 10, with one being the lowest vibration, fear-based emotions rank the lowest. Over time, these dense emotions form a thick wall around the heart, causing an individual to lose contact with his spiritual essence. Entertaining these heavy emotions separates us from the healing stream of Spirit. They could even contribute to physical illness if we hold them long enough. Yes, harboring negative emotions can make you sick. With literally thousands of studies done on the mind-body connection, this is no longer a far-fetched notion.

In contrast, the unifying emotions of gratitude, forgiveness, hopefulness, joy and love resonate with our higher soul-self. Inviting them into our conscious awareness brings lightness to our being by dispelling fear. On the energy scale, these emotions rank the highest. Embracing unifying emotions allows us to live from a heart-centered perspective and in the flow of the Divine. We are revitalized in the process.

I have met with many people who, despite their best efforts, have not forgiven the past and accepted what has occurred. They remain stuck in a time warp of sorts, bound by their own mental constructs and beliefs. Individuals in this emotional predicament come to me with hope of reaching beyond the physical veil and into the spirit world for answers and healing.

The sessions I present in this section—directly transcribed from my tape recordings—illustrate how relationships, despite the pain involved, lead to self-knowledge and, ultimately, to healing for everyone involved. The first four chapters examine the specific emotional impact that the death of a deceased loved one has on surviving family members and friends. The final chapter in this section reveals key spiritual lessons that people have learned from their deceased loved ones.

To protect the identity and privacy of clients, I have changed the names from each session. The only editorial changes that have been made from the original recordings are in respect to the length and clarity of the dialogue. The themes have not been altered. Many of the sessions were done over the phone with individuals from both the United States and around the world. (As I explained earlier, accuracy with phone readings is not compromised because the spirit world is not limited by space or distance.)

My sincere intent is that by sharing these stories, you are inspired to see beyond the difficulties and seeming tragedies of your own life, and to uncover the redeeming spiritual lessons contained within them. If you are struggling with unresolved emotions, perhaps you will be encouraged and strengthened by the wisdom that those on the other side have given in these sessions. Perhaps you will learn about the importance of personal responsibility for your own life choices. Above all, my hope is that you will realize and rejoice in the resiliency and splendor of your own spirit, which transcends all challenges.

* * *

Death is emotionally challenging enough to cope with when a loved one is older or terminally ill. But what if it happens unexpectedly or the deceased one is young? In readings in which the communicating spirits have died under tragic circumstances such as murder, suicide or accident, family members often have unresolved feelings of guilt, anger and confusion that compound their grief. In many of these sessions, spirits bring messages that give insight to surviving family members about the circum-stances surrounding their passing, their emotional state just prior to death and details about the nature of their deaths. These messages offer validation of the soul's survival and comfort in the midst of the family's devastating grief.

Perhaps the greatest challenge that people are faced with following the unexpected death of a loved one is finding an explanation about why such a tragedy would occur. Until peace is found regarding the "why," most people remain emotionally stuck, unresolved and detached from life. Those on the other side recognize this and will come through with information that they hope will alleviate the heaviness and unfinished business around their passing. From their vantage point in spirit, they have a clearer perspective than we do about their death. (As stated earlier, we may not have full knowledge of our own life lessons, let alone someone else's, until we pass into spirit.)

When people die through tragic, untimely circumstances, it may be a result of their own unwise choices, as exercised through their free will. In death by murder, the reason may be rooted in karma—a circumstance that the soul has agreed to experience in order to balance the scales from a former incarnation. Souls who pass into spirit through accidents may have completed life lessons; hence, it is simply time for them to return to spirit. These types of messages are not delivered in every reading but they aren't uncommon, either.

As mentioned previously, the expansiveness that takes place after death gives a comprehensive view of the life just lived. This panoramic life review is the reason that (in cases of suicide, murder and accidents) spirits come through and take responsibility for their choices and actions that led to their demise. This message is communicated to me in readings when I see a clairvoyant image of spirits pointing their fingers at themselves. In many cases, this is the first time that a client "hears" a deceased loved one taking responsibility for their own life or death. Obviously, this accountability helps to alleviate surviving family members' feelings of guilt.

We can all learn from the communication and wisdom that the other side brings through in times of despair. Hopefully, we can use it to heal ourselves and reach out to others through compassion.

A Son's Embrace

When I hear Alison's soft voice on the other end of the phone, I immediately sense a deep well of grief within her. I give her the customary lowdown of how the audio file of her reading would be sent to her email account and advise her to also take notes. I am ready to begin.

I take a breath and focus on what my inner senses are revealing to me. I sense the presence of several male energies who are waiting for the opportunity to speak.

"There is a passing that happened not long ago," I begin. "That's who you want to hear from today, isn't it?"

"Yes, yes," Alison answers softly.

I again focus inward and listen. Instantly I become aware of a strong, insistent presence that steps up to communicate. "One of the males here is very strong," I convey. "He says that you've heard from him on your own, without someone like me."

Alison says nothing. The impressions continue to unfold. "There's also someone who comes through who is a contemporary to you, someone in your generation."

Alison pauses to consider who this other spirit might be. "Oh, yes. There is a contemporary that I asked to come today also."

"This is a spouse or brother to you."

"My brother."

"He says that he wants you to know that he's been helping you with what has happened recently. He wants to make that clear to you."

I feel the presence of the insistent spirit return. "The younger male energy is coming through," I announce.

"Yes," Alison whispers.

"That's who you wanted to hear from, isn't it?"

"Yes."

"Okay, hold on. Your brother is bringing him through. To you, this is either a son or a nephew."

"My son," she says, her voice breaking up.

"Is the rapid passing—here one minute and gone the next—your son?"

"Yes."

At this point I feel Alison's son impress me with calm, reassuring feelings. I do my best to translate this into words. "You need to know that he did not suffer. He makes me feel as if you have questions about that. Have you come to peace with that?"

"I believe I have," Alison responds.

"Okay, but he says in the beginning you had many doubts and questions about his death. He is coming through today and saying he didn't suffer. There is an emphasis on that message. You can now let go of the way his death happened, and the circumstances around it, into a deeper level of acceptance. He's making me feel that not being at peace with how his death happened has caused you additional grief. Does that make sense to you?"

"Yes, it does," she comments in a strained voice.

"Your son is stepping forward and taking some sort of responsibility for his own passing. That doesn't necessarily mean a suicide, only that he did something that contributed to his passing."

"Yes, I understand that."

"He's saying that he didn't listen to you in some way. He's making me feel that you and others tried to talk to him or help him with his life, his circumstances or with his health. I also feel as if there was some sort of emotional heaviness with him. There was some sort of intervention—medical, emotional or psycho-logical—prior to his death."

"Yes, there was."

I suddenly become aware of a fuzzy sensation in my head;

this is the feeling I get from spirits that have used drugs or alcohol. I relay this to Alison, who confirms that her son had abused drugs for years.

"He makes me feel as if his life was a roller coaster ride. There was a period of time when things leveled out for him and then there were times when things were not good. He says that he underwent counseling of some sort and that he sees now—from his vantage point in spirit—that he should have taken better advantage of the help that was offered. You need to know that your son is in a place of healing on the other side. That is where I see him now. When we leave life under painful circumstances— mental, emotional or physical—we get help on the other side."

Alison remains silent on the other end of the phone as she listens to what her son is communicating. The reading continues with an emphatic message from this insistent young man.

"He says that he is doing this [the reading] for you. In the relationship you had with him, you were there for him. He says you were *always* there for him. You didn't fail him or anyone, for that matter. Do you beat yourself up since his passing, believing that you didn't do enough for him?"

"Yes, I have been," Alison confirms, her voice choking with emotion.

"He is emphasizing that you *did* do enough for him. In fact, you actually did *too* much. Your relationship with him feels co-dependent. When we begin to heal, in retrospect, we see that we need to let the other person learn what he needs to learn. He wants you to know that it's okay to realize that you did what you could for him, but that he had emotional problems that were beyond the scope of your control. We can never make another person be who we want him to be. We can only reflect love to others."

Despite the miles between us, I feel Alison's pain. Yet I know the reading can play a significant role in her own healing, as well as her family's and her son in spirit. "I keep feeling that drugs and alcohol played a major part in your son's life. Where does that come in with your family?" I ask.

Without hesitation, Alison says, "Oh, in so many ways!"

"He places that at the top of factors responsible for his passing. He comes through as also having a problem mentally. He kept a lot of emotions inside. He showed a mask to the outside world. There were two sides to him: the one he showed to the outside world and the one he kept inside, private and depressed. He also says he had some legal problems, which were a factor. There were other people in the family who had problems such as his. Do you know who he is referring to?"

"My older son and my brother," Alison answers in a heavy voice.

At that moment, I am impressed by the young man's thoughts that he had done something to hasten his own passing in an effort to end the pain he had been feeling. It isn't clear to me exactly what he means, so I ask Alison for clarification.

"My son's passing was from an overdose," she confirms.

"Ah, I see. That is why he claims responsibility for his own passing. He is apologizing to you for leaving in the way he did. He says there were some attempts to revive him. He saw that because he was still there with his body. Are you the one who found him?"

"Yes, I found him and my husband tried to revive him."

"We don't die alone and even though this passing was unexpected, those in spirit know about it when it happens. They come to help us cross over. The older feminine spirit—the name with the letters M-A-R—came to get him."

"My mom, Marjorie" Alison says, chuckling for the first time. I assumed she was relieved by knowing her mother was with her son.

I feel the presence of my personal spirit guides. They prompt me to talk to Alison about what she can do to move beyond the tragedy of her son's tragic death. "You need to go for counseling.

My guides are showing me a healing group like Compassionate Friends around you. They are saying that your presence is welcome and needed there. As bad as we feel, there is always someone who is worse off or who has had a more recent passing who can benefit from our experience. You will have a lot to offer through this group. There is another person in this group whose son has died in a similar manner who you'll reach out to."

A clairvoyant image of numbers pops into my head. "'What does 1989 mean to you?" I ask.

"That's when my son was born."

"Okay. It's his way of offering validation about the last message he gave you, the one about helping others. He says that he hears you when you play the recorded music for him and also when you talk to him out loud. There is a necklace that he wants to reference, one that's related to him in some way. You hold it in your hand and think about him. Do you understand?"

"Oh, boy, Carole, do I understand that! I feel he led me to get it. It's called a miraculous medal and has the Virgin Mary on it." Alison explains, sobbing again.

"He also shows me an image of a beach and says he felt at peace there. He urges you to go there in the summertime to also find peace."

"Yes, he and I spent many days there together."

"He wants you to remember those days and think of the time you spent with him. That is how he wants you to remember him."

After I deliver several more messages that Alison validates, I feel the young man's energy begin to pull back from the communication. Before he leaves, he impresses me with one last message for his grieving mother.

"Your son shows me a rainbow. He says he will send you signs that he's around through the rainbow."

"I have crystals hanging in the window and when I see a rainbow created from the light coming through them, I stop and say hello to him," Alison replies with emotion in her voice.

As the reading draws to a close, Alison asks if her son wants her to reach out to his friends.

"It's healing for you to talk about your son with his friends, especially the girl that was close to him. Don't be afraid to do that. Helping other people is going to help you. You need to tell his friends about the dangers of drugs. Be honest and direct with people about what happened to your son. In that way, you will help them."

The final message I deliver is a powerful one: "Your son says there was an investigation done into his death, particularly about who gave him the drugs that he overdosed on. I am strongly impressed to tell you that you cannot continue to live every day with the amount of anger you have towards that person. You must do forgiveness work with this and ask Spirit to wash the anger away. Your son was the one responsible for making the decision to take the drugs."

A few months later, Alison contacted me for a follow-up reading in which her son again communicated his presence. I couldn't help but notice how much brighter and clearer Alison was during the second session. I asked her what had changed for her since we last talked. She shared that hearing from her son had given her much needed comfort and an incentive to keep on living, despite her pain.

Recently, she said, "When I hang up the phone from our readings, I feel as if I've really visited with my son. The sessions help ground me back in the physical world during emotional turmoil. I always knew that we lived in both worlds—the physical and the spiritual—but with my son coming through so clearly, that belief has been validated. I'm continuing to attend Alanon meetings. Losing a child has taught me how to live with grief on a daily basis. Hearing from my son has given me strength."

Carry My Story

One beautiful summer evening, Mary and her son, Dan, come to my office for a family session. As is usually the case, I have no idea beforehand who they want to connect with. As they settle into their chairs, I become aware that they are anxious, which I know from experience affects the communication. My spirit guides inspire me to do a short meditation with them to help them relax.

Afterwards, I take a deep breath and begin to focus inward, where I immediately sense the presence of a male energy standing between Mary and Dan. "The older male energy is here. He comes through on your level, Mary. Have you had a contemporary pass?"

Mary thinks for a moment. "My dad."

"No, someone closer in age to you, like a spouse, brother, cousin or friend. That is how this relationship feels to me in terms of the type of relationship you shared. Yes, your dad is here, too."

Again Mary pauses before answering, "No, I can't think of anyone like that."

I try to make sense of what I'm feeling. I ask for clarification. "He presents himself as a friend to you by saying the relationship is on your level instead of a generational distance."

Both Mary and Dan look puzzled. I am also confused by what I am being shown. I decide to move on, hoping this message will eventually make sense to them.

"The name that starts with 'J' is being acknowledged, someone close to you in the family. Do you know who that is, please?"

Dan speaks up. "That's my brother."

"Your grandfather [Mary's dad] wants to pull him into this reading right off the bat. Is he open to this sort of thing? Could you play this recording for him?" I ask.

Both mother and son were silent for a moment.

"No, he's passed," Dan states matter-of-factly.

"Oh! Then this is who your grandfather is bringing through here. *That's* who you wanted to hear from. The contemporary I was feeling is yours, Dan, and not your mother's." I am relieved that things are beginning to fall into place. Apparently, I was feeling a blend of two energies (Mary's father and her late son-Dan's brother) when I started the reading.

I ask my spirit guides to strengthen the communication between the young man in spirit and me. "He passed quickly, just like that," I say, snapping my fingers.

Mary and Dan nod in agreement.

"He makes me feel that there was a problem with alcohol in the family and with him," I continue.

Again, Mary and Dan affirm this.

"He says that one of you tried to talk to him about that. He steps forward now and says he didn't listen to you. Dan, he says he turned his back on you. Now that he has passed, he can see now that you weren't trying to control him, you were trying to help him. He was a rebel, wild, like James Dean. He shows me an image of himself driving too fast in a car that he put parts on from eBay."

"I was just telling my grandma about that the other day!" Dan exclaims. "My brother was always on the Internet buying and selling things. He got large, fancy tires and rims for his car on eBay."

I receive a feeling with the image. "He is using the fast driving as a metaphor for his life: he lived fast and hard. He didn't really care about things. He claims responsibility for that now. Mary, you and he had angry, harsh words prior to this passing. You tried to reach out to him but you couldn't. I'm being shown a clairvoyant image of you crying and feeling as if you had no idea how to help him."

Mary's eyes fill with tears as she listens to the messages from her son in spirit. What I feel coming next from J is difficult yet necessary to say to Mary and Dan. I take a deep breath.

"I'm going to be very direct in telling you that your son has regrets about his life. He didn't pay attention to advice that you gave him. He wants me to stress to you that he is sorry and he admits that he was wrong. That message is for both of you. You may have waited a long time to hear that, even though the passing doesn't feel as if it happened that long ago."

Mary cries softly. Suddenly I feel that J impresses me with the sensation of an impact in my head. "The strong impact in the head, does that make sense to you? Is that how he passed?"

Both mother and son stare at me in astonishment. Finally Dan says in a flat voice: "Yeah, he shot himself in the head." Mary looks down and continues to cry.

My heart fills with compassion for this family who obviously suffered tremendously from losing one of their own to suicide. "I'm sorry. I know this is hard for you, but you are here to heal. He says that you had inklings, Mary, about this happening before it actually did. He says there were some signs you received about it beforehand and that it was not totally unexpected, although it was shocking."

Mary nods in agreement.

"There is someone in the family who lives in a trailer or mobile home."

"His dad- my ex-husband. He and I are divorced now," Mary shares.

"The gun he used to kill himself was my dad's," Dan offers.

J seems to want to talk about his father, especially about the relationship between his parents. "Your son gives me a feeling as if your ex-husband has felt responsible and guilty about J's passing because of the gun being his. He shows me a large cloud of guilt over his father's head. Have you talked to him, Mary?"

"We don't talk anymore. I blame him for Josh's passing."

"Oh, that is what he is trying to say then! What he means is that his dad is guilty in your eyes. There is a closed door emotionally between you and him, much anger and pain."

Mary nodded.

I continue with the impressions I am receiving, which come primarily through feelings. The next message rings through loud and clear, and I attempt to deliver it with as much emphasis as I can.

"Josh does not want you to blame his father for his death. Do you remember at the start of the reading when he said he was responsible for the way he lived his life? The truth is that no one can make us do anything. That realization is part of the healing process for both of you. Start the forgiveness process today, which alleviates you from the terrible burden of anger and resentment. By the way, he says that Dad is dealing with his pain by drinking."

"Yes, he started to drink after Josh's death," Mary responds with a grimace.

"Send him prayers. It will release both of you from the toxic anger that you have."

"Josh wants you to know he is getting help on the other side."

Images of tattoos appear in my mind. I describe these to Mary and Dan.

Mary lifts her sleeve and proudly reveals a tattoo that she got in her late son's memory. Dan chimes in and says that he also got one in his brother's memory.

"He kids you about changing your mind about which one you wanted."

"Yeah, I did," Dan smiles.

I listen for another message from Josh. The next impression I receive concerns someone from Josh's generation, a female. No other information is forthcoming. I relay this to Mary and Dan.

After much hesitation, Dan reveals, "Well, this was a murder-suicide case."

I am temporarily stunned by this sudden revelation. "So, there was a female who passed as well? He murdered her?"

"Uh-huh, it was his girlfriend. They were engaged."

"You need to know she is also receiving healing on the other side. You *do* understand that their relationship was volatile before this happened, right? He says there was a protection from abuse order taken out against him."

"Yes," Mary affirms. "But why did he do what he did?"

Her question hangs in the air between us. I focus within to hear more from Josh. "He makes me feel as if there was an argument prior to the incident. There was an accusation of something. Someone was unfaithful. They should not have been together. There was hardcore substance abuse in addition to alcohol. That is what he is saying you tried to warn him about, Mary. He shows me newspaper clippings that you have about all of this."

"Yes," Mary responds. "His girlfriend had been unfaithful to him."

The next message Josh delivers is about his children. "He says they may need counseling. I'm strongly impressed to tell you that if you don't address this now, his son, in particular, could carry anger and pain. It would be good to get him evaluated."

Near the end of the session, I ask if they have any questions. After a few moments of silence, Dan looks at me and says in a strained voice: "This is hard for me, you know." I sense the overwhelming sadness within him.

"I know it is. I cannot say that I know how you feel because I have not had this sort of event happen to me. But I can share with you two things that I've learned from doing this work for many years: First, we don't die. Your brother lives on in spirit. Second, you and your family need to continue to send him prayers because he's still in an acclimation period on the other side. He's still getting counseling and making restitution on a spiritual level for what he's done. I strongly encourage you to open a spiritual connection if you don't already have one."

Mary and Dan listen intently.

"Your brother, Dan, encourages you to share what happened

to him with other young people so they don't go down the road he did. He says you will carry his story. That is how you can take something extremely tragic and turn it into something more positive."

Before we part, I encourage Mary and Dan to continue to send Josh prayer to help him with much needed healing in the spirit world. After the session, I notice that their energy is lighter and higher than when they had arrived. They not only received confirmation from Josh that he was alive in spirit, but also spiritual guidance about how to transcend the devastating events that had taken place. Losing a son and brother had shattered their lives. I could only hope they would take his advice to find something redeeming from the tragedy. As I write this, I send a special prayer of healing their way.

You Are Not Alone

The following session is a good example of how souls in spirit must come to terms with unresolved emotions in order to be at peace. It illustrates how releasing old wounds happens for not only those in spirit, but also for their loved ones in the physical world who hear from them. This catharsis is necessary for each to move forward spiritually.

Bonnie, a soft-spoken, attractive woman in her 40's, tells me she was referred to me by one of her friends who had a reading. After saying my prayer, I ask her what she wants from the session: insights about her life, contact with the spirit world or a combination of both.

"I really don't know," she murmurs. "I'm in a bad state. I can't find a psychiatrist or therapist who can help me. I need healing," she says, looking deeply into my eyes.

"Have you gone that route already?" I ask for clarification.

"Yes. The reason I'm here is because I had someone close to me die."

I feel Bonnie's immense, unresolved pain as I sit with her. In my mind, I flash back to the meditation I always do before readings. I had been impressed to call on Archangel Raphael (who works with healing energy) to be with me in Bonnie's session. I share this with her and assure her that this powerful angel is indeed working with her through our session. I then tune into her feelings.

"This passing might not have been that recent, but it feels recent because you are still there in an emotional sense. You know, when this person died, a part of you left. Haven't you made the statement that when the death happened, a part of you was gone, too?"

Bonnie draws in her breath. "Yes, I have."

"I'm feeling as if you did not want to go on living. One of the things I've learned from communicating with the spirit world is that those on the other side want us to go on with our lives. That honors them. I feel as if your energy is trapped in the past, when the passing happened. You must pull it forward into the present moment, where healing can happen."

The reading continues to address Bonnie's feelings. "You've been encouraged by friends and family to release the past and begin to live again. But there is a lot of resistance within you to doing that. You want to continually revert to the past as if you are repeatedly saying, 'But look what happened'!"

"I know. I can't get over it," Bonnie says quietly.

"You need to know that Spirit is within you and the connection with those on the other side is eternal. You've asked if you will see loved ones again when you cross over. But you don't have to wait until then because you can make a connection with them through your inner senses, the same ones used when I do readings."

After the delivery of this message, I feel someone coming through who passed quickly and unexpectedly. I am not certain of the spirit's relationship with Bonnie, but I pass it along to her. She validates that she knows this to be true. "That's a big part of why you can't let go," I continue. "It was as if the wind was knocked out of you. In reality, this death was more like a *tornado*."

"Yes," Bonnie whispers.

I continue to listen within. "He's making me feel as if his head and chest area are related to his death. It feels like a quick jolt of some sort. I hope this makes sense."

Bonnie concurs.

I continue to describe what I am feeling from the spirit. "He's presenting himself as younger than you, although he makes me feel as if he is your friend, also. He's with another male who is older. He wants you to know he's not alone. His personality comes through as being laid back. Is this your son?"

"Yes."

"Well, he says that he did some stupid things in his life and that he can see that now. He shows me a large question mark over your head regarding his passing and an image of a newspaper. There must have been an article written about his death."

"Yes! Yes!"

By this time, it's apparent why Bonnie is having such an intense struggle with unresolved grief. A parent is never the same after the loss of a child. But there was more. The passing felt tragic and unresolved- further reason for Bonnie's emotional turmoil.

"He says that there was a police investigation done into his death and that you've also looked into some things on your own. He gives me a bad feeling about other people he associated with. You've talked to some of them after his death and they tried to wash their hands of any involvement with his death, a cover-up. Further, he says that you need to follow your gut as far as what you suspect because it is true."

The story coming from Bonnie's son continues to unfold in my head. "The other people he mentions are in trouble legally. They are in jail, where they belong. There's a sense of justice that will be done. He says you will have more emotional closure and peace about his death."

"I hope so," Bonnie sighs.

"Do you know why he would be showing me a wooded area that is near you?"

"I just spent time there last night! I go there because it is a way that I connect with him. He and I used to do that when he was young."

"And there is a large tree he makes reference to."

"Last night I spent time near a dogwood tree and I thought of him. I believe that is what he's saying."

"He was there with you. There's an engraving somehow connected to the tree. Do you know what he means?"

For the next five minutes, Bonnie and I go back and forth trying to understand where this perplexing message fits in. I ask her son for clarification but the message remains the same about the engraving somehow being connected with the tree. Finally, Bonnie remembers that a tree had been planted in his memory at the school where her son had worked as a teacher. The school board was planning to place an engraved plaque next to it.

"Your son shows me that his life went quite well for a long period of time and then there is a turn for the worst, an abrupt change. This was a pivotal point and a downward spiral as far as he is concerned. He comes through with regrets about that. He says it's not your fault. He doesn't want you to carry that burden."

"Yes, I know. That's true about his life taking a wrong turn when he got involved with people who brought him down," Bonnie replies.

"I'm shown trophies and certificates that he had. You've recently looked at those. He was a mentor for others, he says. There was recognition and a scholarship for football. His death shocked many people who knew him."

"There were hundreds! He had gone to college on a football scholarship." Bonnie confirms.

Suddenly I am filled with a profound sense of regret. "Your son says he's sorry. Very simply, he's sorry."

Upon hearing this, Bonnie cries.

"He wants to wipe the slate clean. Underneath it, there is much heartfelt energy and sincerity. He says he never meant for his life to go badly. He can see how he wasted his life. I hope this all makes sense to you."

"It does."

"Well, there is a lot of emotion and tragedy connected with his passing."

"Yes. I used to feel him around me when he first passed. It's been a long time since I've felt him."

"You feel him around your neck and shoulders. He does that to comfort you," I confirm. "He'll also come to you through music, the visual recordings you have of him and birds. These are all signs he'll give you."

"Is he happy?" Bonnie asks in a soft voice.

It was a question I've been asked many times before in readings. Instead of simply saying "yes" or "no," I explain to Bonnie that being in spirit is not the same type of happiness we have on the physical plane. In spirit, souls return to their pure form along with the experience and knowledge of the life just lived. Sometimes counseling is required in order to assimilate unfinished lessons from the former life. Unresolved feelings of guilt, anger, sadness and shame block souls' progress on the other side. These dense emotions must be worked through and released. Happiness in spirit comes from souls' sense of completeness through the recognition of themselves as the Divine. It is a return to love in the purest sense.

"Your son says he's around children on the other side and that's he doing teaching over there."

"That makes sense since he was a teacher in life. That's good to know."

"I'm being shown a book with writing, a dedication, in the front of it. It's somehow related to your son. Do you know what this means?"

Bonnie's face lights up. "Our state representative sent it to us in his memory. It was for being an outstanding citizen and teacher."

At this point, I feel Bonnie's son pull back from me, signaling that the communication is coming to a close. "All of this has been your son's way of coming through to you here tonight. He hands you roses as a symbol of his unconditional love for you."

One hour after Bonnie arrived in my office, her demeanor has remarkably changed from one of despondency to hopefulness. The young man gave indisputable, validating details about his life and uplifting messages to ease his mother's suffering. Although the exact manner of his death is not apparent from the reading, Bonnie confirmed that the cause of her son's death was not clear; the family suspected drugs may have been involved, although it had not been proven through an autopsy. Before she leaves, we chat about her late son's accomplishments and her plans for the future. She tells me she is grateful and relieved to know that her son is undoubtedly around her, and that he is continuing with his work in spirit. Before she leaves, Bonnie gives me a warm embrace. Her son's enduring love was a beacon of hope for her, guiding her into a new day.

Mom, It's Time to Let Go!

The following transcript is taken from a phone session I did with Evelyn who was referred to me by another client. This reading illustrates the reunion between mother and son, who delivers insightful messages about his death by murder and his mother's need to move beyond it through forgiveness.

"The first person stepping through is one who comes with a father's energy," I begin. "There are several different spirits who are here for you tonight. There is a connection with a man related to you who had a laboring, physical sort of job because he wore casual attire when he did his work—specifically, a white tee-shirt."

"That could be either my father or my son," Evelyn replies in an excited voice.

"Hold on," I say, as I tune in to get a clearer picture. "Yes, it's clearly a white tee-shirt he has on. This is the way he wants to identify himself because he says you would recognize him in that way."

"My son *always* wore sleeveless white tee-shirts to work," Evelyn quickly responds.

"Okay. He comes through here strongly. That must be who you want to hear from today." More detail about Evelyn's son unfolds in my mind.

"He's ruggedly built, muscular, from the type of work he did. He says you asked him to come here. He says he is doing this for you to be able to let go. This message is strongly emphasized. There is a feeling here of extra doses of grief and tragedy connected with his death. Does that make sense?"

"Yes, it does."

At this point, I am infused with feelings of turmoil and anger around this man's passing. I don't know if it is connected to the way he died or how his family feels as a result of his death. I relay this to Evelyn.

"He says there was a legal situation around his death and that you are still having ramifications from this."

Evelyn pauses. "Well, it's over legally but in my heart it is not."

"I know. That is what he means by saying he is doing this to help you to let go. It doesn't mean that you will let go of *him*. What it means is that in order for you to have peace, you must relinquish the strong emotions about how he died. Regarding the legal reference he made earlier, there is a feeling that justice has not been done. Was this a murder?"

"Yes," Evelyn confirms.

"He makes me feel that he left in a very turbulent way." Suddenly I'm impressed with more communication by the young man. "Wait, there is more. His death was publicized in the news. There was a deep betrayal here and a feeling that someone who knew him did him in."

"Yes, there was," Evelyn interjects. "He was set up," she announced firmly.

"He says he was ambushed. He was the fall guy." This spirit's thoughts are coming through so quickly and excitedly that I mentally ask him to slow down his communication. I feel that he desperately wants his mother to find peace about his death.

"The people who murdered him he had once considered friends. He got involved with the wrong people who betrayed him."

"Yes, he thought they were his friends but they weren't."

"There was a robbery connected with this as far as the others were concerned. They robbed places to get drugs and that was involved with his passing, as well. They wanted what he had. He says he was at the wrong place at the wrong time. There was someone present there who was very deceptive and had an alias, another name."

"Spike!" Evelyn gasps. "Ask my son about the name Spike! He was involved!"

I intuitively feel the man in spirit validate the name. "There are feelings of competition and jealousy between this man and your son. Is this man in jail?"

"None of the people involved went to jail. All of them stuck together in their story. At the trial, the prosecutor told us that a dead man can't talk. Spike was jealous because my son dated his ex-wife," she confirms.

"Oh, that is why he says justice wasn't done. I see. Your son insists they were the ones who killed him. Hold on while I again tell him to slow down his rapid-fire thoughts." I pause and silently request this. In a minute, I feel the communication slowing down. I take a breath and continue the reading.

"He says there was an argument and confrontation that preceded his death. Did they bring that out in court?"

"No, but I heard that through hearsay."

My spirit guides gently impress me to direct the reading away from discussing the circumstances of Evelyn's son's death and move it toward helping Evelyn to heal painful emotions about his death.

"In the remaining time we have in our session, I'd like to talk with you about forgiveness. Let me clarify what that really means on a spiritual level. Forgiveness doesn't mean that what was done to your son was fine and dandy. Rather, it means that you don't want to carry the extreme bitterness, hatred or anger about your son's death. From the other side, the perspective is larger and that picture gives you reason to move on with your life. Your life stopped when your son died."

"Yes." Evelyn begins to choke up.

"That is completely understandable. Now, however, you must pull the energy of yourself that you left in the past forward- into the present. You need to call on Archangel Raphael to help heal your heart. I'm to tell you that your son is getting help on the other side because he left with emotional and mental imbalances. He comes through as being very agitated."

"Yes, that's right, he was. He has a son with a woman who has lots of troubles. I'm raising the child now."

"You need to be in a better place emotionally because you're the mother of this child now. You must come into a deeper sense of peace. That is only possible through making a spiritual connection, whether through Jesus, Buddha, Krishna or just a higher power. It doesn't matter but it must be outside of you to get rid of these terrible feelings. I'm impressed to suggest that you also go to counseling. You have been overwhelmed for many years. I feel compelled to tell you to take care of yourself. Energy has been drained from you that you must restore. Your son is pointing to your legs, knees and feet."

"Oh, yes! I'm so tired," Evelyn says sighing loudly. "My legs and feet hurt me daily."

"It's best to take care of yourself because heavy, stressful emotions will eventually take their toll on the physical body. This has been your son's way of coming through to you. You can connect with him anytime without me through the bond of love."

The reading concludes with several evidentiary messages about Evelyn's grandson from his dad in spirit. Before we hang up, Evelyn cries softly as she thanks me. I feel her pain, but know she has the strength within to overcome it. For a few minutes after the call, I sit and ponder what had been communicated in the reading. I wondered how people successfully cope with a catastrophic occurrence such as the murder of their own child. The only conceivable way had to be through acknowledging the healing presence of Spirit. It was the end of the day and I was tired, yet I felt fulfilled in knowing that much-needed healing- in the form of spiritual awareness- had been delivered in the short span of the last session. As I closed shop for the day, I was grateful to be a small part of this woman's personal journey into greater spiritual understanding and peace.

Five

Finding Peace

I will be still an instant and go home.
A Course in Miracles Workbook for Students, **Lesson 182**

If forgiveness is the cornerstone of all healing, why do we resist doing it? Is forgiveness something we must learn to do in order to mature spiritually? Since the beginning of time, human beings have committed injustices towards one another. How can such acts possibly be forgiven if we are harmed by someone's words or actions?

As stated earlier, I believe many people misinterpret what forgiveness actually means. Simply stated, it is letting go mentally and emotionally of the past. In essence, we detach from emotions such as anger, resentment, jealousy, betrayal and sorrow that have become too weighty to carry. By doing so, we enter into the grace, purity and truth of Spirit within ourselves and others. This is the only reality there is, since Spirit can never be diminished or destroyed by anything we do, say or think. It can only be temporarily obscured from our conscious awareness when we choose to separate ourselves from it through un-forgiving thoughts and attitudes.

Forgiveness does *not* mean that we are condoning the affront in whatever form it has taken place, nor does it mean that we place ourselves in the same line of fire to re-experience similar circumstances. It means simply that we make a choice to identify with the only truth that sets us free: the Divine within each person. If our intent is to focus on this redeeming resource within ourselves and others, we have to detach from thoughts and feelings that emanate from the ego, which separate us from the higher, unifying force within.

At times, we may mistakenly believe that if we let go of our feelings towards an injustice that another has done, they will somehow escape punishment. We sometimes incorrectly (and egotistically) assume that it is our duty to see to it that others live in the prison of condemnation, even if it exists only in our own mind. But it is not our role to punish another; cosmic justice (karma) always exists, despite our ignorance or denial of it. What we sow, we reap. If we engage in judgment of others, we demonstrate a lack of faith in the innate perfection and goodness of this universal law, which works like a boomerang, so to speak. That is, judging others guarantees that we will be judged. Hating others means we will experience hatred directed at ourselves. On the other hand, if we forgive, we release the repercussions of holding such toxic thought and emotions. We instead acknowledge and trust in the perfection of universal law and Spirit. The boomerang will then return all of these uplifting qualities to us.

When we forgive, we do so from the perspective that the "guilty" person made choices from the level of consciousness (based on their beliefs) that they were operating from at the time. If one doesn't know any better- given his level of consciousness- how can one choose a different path? Beliefs, because they are generated by our minds, are subjective and at the discretion of our own minds. They are repetitive thoughts we have chosen to give energy to-not supreme reality. The one underlying Truth- surpassing all beliefs- is the all-encompassing unity of Spirit, the one eternal source of all being.

As you will see in the stories in this chapter, forgiveness (releasing the past) can transform relationships and heal generations of pain. My hope is that you too, come home through Spirit to find peace.

Lifting the Heaviness of Anger

I chose the following session because it is representative of others I've done in which people's anger towards a deceased family prevents them from having emotional closure and peace of mind. The reading also focuses on several key points central to forgiveness: the awareness of self beyond the personality, karma as "letting go" of the past, and the use of specific techniques in the process of achieving true forgiveness.

"What do you want me to focus on today: mediumship or life issues?" I ask Kathy over the phone.

"I had a very difficult marriage with my late ex-husband, John," she begins. "My son, John, and I went to see him when he was in the hospital, dying from cancer. I was with him for a week, by his request, and he seemed happier than I'd ever known him. Even though things had been rough between us, I really enjoyed that time with him. But then I found out after he died that he left everything, a very large estate, to his girlfriend of six years. My four sons and I were so hurt by that. I was very angry that he would treat his sons in this way. This has turned into a huge mess. My sons have gone to court to contest the will. I'm wondering if he would come through today and say anything about all of this."

"Let's see what happens," I respond as I begin to focus inward.

I'm immediately prompted to mention the emotional dynamics of Kathy's situation. "The emotional aspects of the relationship the two of you had are coming up for you because of the court case," I begin. "When that is finished, the emotional cycle will be complete, and the karma between the two of you will be finished, also. You won't have to repeat these spiritual lessons anymore. Even though you were divorced years ago, the emotional energy was still being carried, especially through your children."

"I see," Kathy responds.

"The reason why you saw a difference in John when he was dying was because the dying process brought him into presence, or spiritual awareness. He had a very strong, controlling personality and . . . "

"Oh my gosh, yeah," Kathy quickly interrupts.

"When people are dying, sometimes, there is a profound spiritual awareness that is created," I continue. "We become aware that we are more than our personality and body. He called for you to be there with him as some sort of acceptance or closure emotionally. Part of your healing is to realize that he finally understood how he had treated you and the boys. He became aware that he needed to make things right, if you know what I mean."

"Yes."

"That last time you had with him is what you need to focus on since it is what he is in now. Let me explain. When we cross over, we are shown our life in a review. John had already started to go into that perspective when he was dying. That's why he called for you to come. His ego had begun to drop off. He had one foot on the other side and one with his physical presence here. What will help you in coming to emotional closure now is for you to understand that he wanted to wipe the slate clean from the past. You don't want to carry the lack of forgiveness anymore, do you?"

"Right."

"The fact that you had gotten divorced from him means that you chose to not repeat these emotional patterns with him anymore. In a spiritual sense, that is forgiveness. You wanted to let it go. The minute that we say, 'I don't want to carry it anymore' is the minute healing begins."

I suddenly see in my mind's eye the image of a balanced scale, a symbol representing justice. I share this with Kathy and add that John is communicating through this symbol that justice (as far as her sons are concerned) would be done in the court case.

"He makes me feel that the will your sons are contesting will be turned around in their favor."

"Does he say how he feels about what has happened in our lives since he died?"

"He gives me the sense that he is helping from the spirit world for the right thing to be done. He shows me that there was much manipulation on the part of his girlfriend."

"I've felt that."

"When someone imposes her will on a situation, there's always a balancing that must occur. If, for some reason, things wouldn't work out for your sons, rest assured that karma is operating here. This woman has imposed selfishness and that must be balanced by her. There's always personal responsibility involved. Your husband has seen that. He's also seen the repercussions of his own behavior toward you and his sons. There is not an outside, punishing God; we always punish ourselves."

"Uh-huh," Kathy agrees.

"You've already done much healing around this relationship."

"I've worked on it for years!"

"Spirit is showing me that there's been a lot of letting go on your part. The karmic lessons that came up for you through this relationship were self-worth, patience and faith. These are spiritual energies. Relationships are always reflecting some aspect of self to us, even though there is another individual involved. You won't have to go through the same lessons again."

"Good!" Kathy's relief was palpable through the phone line.

"The lawsuit is the last root of the karmic themes you are learning. It's another level of forgiveness for you. No one ever really triumphs when one's will is inflicted upon another. His girlfriend won't feel joy even if she would win the estate because there's too much ego and selfishness attached to it."

"Yes, I agree. My husband died without dignity because of the friends he had and the circumstances surrounding his signing of his will. John (her son) saw all of that going on when he was around his dad at the end of his life."

"I'm hearing the word 'duress.' Your ex-husband makes me feel that he was under stress when he signed his will. He wasn't of clear mind."

"I know that the people around him withheld his medication until he signed things. That's duress, I suppose!"

"Oh, yes. It will take proof that this happened, but it will be done, he says. This is not an easy time for you but it is necessary that it happens."

"The boys were very good to him all of his life. For him to turn his back on them . . . well, it hurt them very much."

"He makes me feel as if he did not intend that. There was much outside influence in regards to his will. He was not in his right mind. I also feel that he had lost his capacity to reason."

"I believe his alcoholism played a large part."

"Yes and he says he did not die sober."

"Right, he never was."

After I give messages about another circumstance in Kathy's life, the reading refocuses on her relationship with her ex-husband.

"I feel I need to get away from all of this family stuff when the court case is finished," Kathy shares. "I tend to do too much for my family. I really think I need to withdraw for several months."

"Yes, because that awareness to withdraw is signaling the end of the cycle, indicating that you need not go back over the same emotional territory again and again. I urge you to do some sort of forgiveness ritual around your relationship with John."

"I thought I had forgiven him and then when he did this with the will, I was enraged. That made me realize there's still something left I need to do."

"Yes, anger is the last root as far as the emotional charge between the two of you. Feel the anger but don't attach to it. Let it pass through you," I advise Kathy.

"I try to focus on the last week we had together. We laughed and talked."

"That's how you need to remember him. He had recognition before he passed that he needed to make closure with you. Keep that in your heart when the anger comes up. He says he knows about your feelings."

"Okay."

"As far as rituals go, write a letter with your feelings and take it outside to burn it. Release it. Let it go. Say a prayer as you put the match to it. Do a body cleanse in water, which is symbolic of your anger being washed away in spiritual awareness. Call on Archangel Michael to help you cut cords from the past."

"He's my favorite angel. I've called on him before."

The reading concludes shortly after giving final messages about how Kathy can continue her healing process in the days ahead. At this point, I feel confident that she now has an expanded understanding of the difficult, problematic relationship she had shared with her late husband. This newfound, elevated perspective transcended the consuming anger that had held her hostage for so long and freed her from holding resentment toward her late husband's girlfriend. Despite his death, their relationship continued to serve as a catalyst for her spiritual growth. In that awareness, both were renewed.

Our Love is with You, Mom

While meditating before the following phone reading, I ask Archangel Raphael to be present for the session. At the time, I have no way of knowing that the woman I am about to connect with had lost both her daughter and son in the span of a few years. Nor did I know that in the reading, she would unexpectedly hear from a young man who didn't like or respect her when he was alive. I only knew that I intuitively felt that the session would be emotionally heavy and that this powerful angel could help ease the burden.

"I prepared for this all week," Jen announces before I say my opening prayer. "I wrote questions and meditated as you suggested."

She sounds good, I ponder, yet I know better than to distrust that my intuition had prompted me to call in extra healing energy. I silently ask Spirit to remove my expectations about the reading. I soon discover why.

"Spirit is making me feel that you have been going through a huge transition for some time. There is so much that you are healing right now. When that happens, we are removing our old ways of being. A door has slammed shut for you. There's a need for you to understand that you're not alone and that you are being helped from the other side."

Jen is silent. I continue.

"There have been several significant passings, people who were very close to you. The older male on your dad's side is here for you. He comes through with a very protective stance towards you."

"That's my grandpa!"

"He is bringing through the younger male energy, younger than him, to you. The reason why your grandfather is coming through first is to let you know this other soul is with him. You've asked, 'Who is he with?' Your grandfather acts as a guardian for him."

On the other end of the phone, I can hear Jen start to cry. I continue giving the impressions I am receiving. "Is this your child?"

"Yes." Jen seems to have regained her emotional composure.

"This was a quick passing and very abrupt. He was here one minute and gone the next. There was something emotionally abrupt about it, as well. It feels as though there was something unfinished emotionally with him before his death. Hmm . . . I don't where he's taking me with this feeling. There were difficulties before he died. This may have involved someone else in the family. Had he been estranged from you or the family?"

"You mean emotionally?"

"Yes," I respond.

"Well, I lost my daughter a year prior and he was very upset by her loss," Jen answers, her voice breaking up.

I instantly become aware of the enormous pain Jen has been enduring. I visualize Archangel Raphael sending brilliant, green rays of healing to her. "You've lost two children. I want to see if your daughter comes through here, as well. The emotional stuff—that's where your son wants to go with this reading. There's a feeling of isolation and shutting down I feel with you. I hate to say it but had you at some point thought about going to the other side yourself?"

"Yes."

"He says that after she passed, he helped you through that. Then, when he passed, you felt as if you lost the only support you had at the time."

"Yes."

"Number nine or September is relevant to you or the family. I also feel someone died accidentally."

"September is my youngest daughter's {still alive} birthday. Both my son and other daughter died in accidents."

"He wants to include your youngest daughter in this reading. He says she needs to hear from him, too. Let's go back to the message about your emotions. Your son makes me feel that when you wanted to die, he was instrumental in helping and supporting you."

"He saved me," Jen says with quiet intensity.

"His presence for you was not only life-saving, it was angelic. He emphasizes for you to stay on your medication for depression and to continue with therapy. That's what he wants you to do."

"I will," she promises.

Several minutes pass in which I give identification of other family members and friends. "A name that starts with S-H is coming through."

Jen is silent for a moment. "I don't know who that is."

"I'm hearing Shawn or Shane."

"Shawn! He was my [late] daughter's boyfriend. They each had two children. He died over a year ago."

"Do you mean your daughter who passed?"

"Yes. Shawn hated me. I tried to be everything I could for him, but . . . "

"Well, his personality feels very self-absorbed. I feel something about drugs with him."

"He didn't take them but he sold them."

"Okay. You've done forgiveness around this issue. I feel this is also your daughter's way of coming through here, as well. Shawn has seen how he acted and his coming through today is his way of making amends to you."

"I've prayed for him and forgiven him."

"In the relationship between him and your daughter, I feel there was emotional abuse. At some point, you tried to help her."

"Yes, I did, but Shawn's sister was awarded custody of the kids."

"Okay, hold on while I get more information." I pause to ask Shawn for clarification around the situation. "If there had been a relationship between you and the kids before, your daughter says there will be an opportunity for that to come back together. You've prayed for that."

"That would be very nice," Jen says in a strained voice.

"Hadn't you felt that the sister took them away from you because she didn't want anything to do with your side of the family? This was an estrangement. She used them as pawns."

"Oh my God! This is amazing! Yes!"

"She was reacting out of fear and selfishness. Your prayers will help with a reunion with one of the children. The month of August is being mentioned with that."

As the communication with Jen's son, daughter and her

boyfriend continues, I have to depend on Jen to assign the messages to each as they come through because it is somewhat confusing for me. "Someone says he did something really stupid that caused his passing. Which one would that be?"

"That would be Shawn. After my daughter passed, he kept overeating. I tried to get him on different diets. He wouldn't listen. He died of complications from obesity."

"He's admitting that he should have listened. You never would have heard that when he was here. He's now saying you were right. His purpose here today is healing for both of you. He says he committed a slow suicide by overeating since he was diabetic. You've wanted to release the past and invite forgiveness into your life. He realizes that."

"It's true, he was a diabetic!"

"You can rest in knowing that with all three souls, you did the very best you could. You wanted better for your daughter but she made her own choices. She understands your love for her. The month of April is mentioned."

"That's when she died."

"That's a validation that's it her," I assure her.

Other messages follow from Jen's children. "Your son says you talked to him out loud when you had private viewing time with his body. He's saying he heard that. He shows me a polo shirt with three buttons on it and an embroidered insignia on the pocket."

"Yes. It was a sport shirt he wore a lot."

"Do you still have it?"

"It's in front of me right now."

I am astounded by the accuracy of the message. Jen's son clearly wants her to know he is right there with her. "You have it in front of you now? That's very interesting. That's why he's showing it to me. He's a good communicator. He says there's a dog with him. This dog used to catch things in his mouth."

"Our German shepherd, Chief, passed right after him," Jen

says sniffling. "He loved to catch a Frisbee."

"Your son was a caretaker. He also did community service."

"Yes, he did," Jen says, laughing.

I am relieved that the heavy part of the reading seems to be receding. "He shows me a medal he won for his service."

"Yes!"

"A huge message from him to you today is for you to be at peace. He wants you to be able to carry on. You felt safe with him."

"I always felt safe with my son. Since he's passed, I've felt so alone."

"There's a need for you to have a support group. This may come through your counseling."

Near the end of the reading, Jen asks whether her son and daughter have given her signs to let her know they are around.

"You'll find coins in places you wouldn't expect. Your son comes through by touch. I call them hugs from heaven. This will be in your kitchen."

"Can he verify how he died?" Jen asks.

I focus inward as an image appears in my mind. "I see a written report about his death."

"Yes, there was."

"He makes me feel that the report is accurate. He says he was in the wrong place at the wrong time. He says that his passing was totally unexpected. There was someone else involved in his death."

"Yes, but they never pressed charges against him."

"He makes me feel that at some point they will."

Just before the reading closes, Jen says, "You've helped me immensely today."

"I know that you are held in the arms of Spirit. I'll leave that with you." I hang up and take a deep breath to disconnect from the energy.

For a few days, that reading stuck with me. I could not fathom how people like Jen deal with losing two children, except by the exceptional grace and healing of Spirit. I tried to imagine how much fortitude it must take to navigate through such loss. I also considered how startling Shawn's unexpected presence in the reading must have been for her. Above all, I was profoundly grateful that I was able to reunite Jen with her children and help to bring her peace.

A few months ago, Jen emailed to tell me about further validations from the reading that she had since uncovered. She also asked for my insights about several intriguing incidents that happened since the reading. We both felt that these were communications from her children in spirit. One thing became certain to me: In the aftermath of tremendous tragedy, Jen was attempting to move on with her life, supported by the bond of love she and her children still share.

The Man with Angel Wings

Often, when I attempt to (unknowingly) connect with spirits who have committed suicide, I hit a brick wall with the communication. In these cases, a connection may not happen or it will be unclear, much to the dismay of both clients and myself. In many instances, souls who have taken their own lives do not want to reconnect with the specific circumstances of their passing and so may not convey this information to me. Years ago when this would happen, I thought I was having an "off" day. With the counsel of my spirit guides, I've come to understand that this blockage is due to the density of the emotional energy (depression, mental illness or hopelessness) that these spirits had in life, especially at the time of death; however, good communication is possible if spirits have begun working through some of these heavy emotions on the other side. As you will see in the next session, part of that healing involves the release of unfinished business with the family left behind. Going into the session, I had no knowledge that the man whom my client wanted to connect with (her brother) had taken his own life.

Cathy, a soft- spoken, pretty woman in her forties, is sitting on the edge of her seat during the half hour we are spending together. She also keeps her eyes closed for most of the reading, which I assume is to focus on what I am saying.

"I'm interested in how my brother is doing," she states calmly when I ask why she has come for a reading. "I'd also like to hear from other relatives."

I explain that I have no idea if her brother will come through and that the best results come when people remain open and hopeful. Then I recite my prayer.

The reading begins with Cathy's in-laws clearly identifying themselves. Soon after, I am impressed with what to say: "I'm being told that you're an emissary of truthfulness. What I mean is that you get to the bottom of things and make sure the right thing is done. I feel that this somehow applies to you and your family."

"Yes, I know what you mean by that," Cathy replies.

"Someone is making me feel that this especially applies to your brother. You were the truth seeker, the one who dug in and got things out in the open and made things right."

I access that the messages are hitting home with Cathy. She nods her head and says, "I just don't know if he ever understood what I tried to do to help him."

"He does now. He wants you to know he is aware of that. I see him in a healing place on the other side. He's undergone a dramatic spiritual awakening since he's passed. You need to know he's pointing at himself, indicating he's taking responsibility for his own death."

Upon hearing this, Cathy shifts slightly in her seat. "Yes," she replies with her eyes still closed.

"He didn't accept responsibility when he was here, but he is now. You tried to show him that. He says, 'You were always there, no matter what.' Even though you weren't there all the time physically, you were there in the spirit of love. Now, he returns that to you by being with *you* in spirit."

Cathy's face is expressionless as she listens.

The next message seems so ridiculous to me that, at first, I wait a few seconds to consider whether I should speak it. Remembering my commitment to not censor information during readings, I decide to go for it.

"This is funny, but he says he's grown his angel wings," I say with a laugh. "I don't normally hear that from spirits. That has something to do with a tribute. Do you understand this?" I half expect that she will burst into laughter.

But surprisingly Cathy is not confused by the message. "Yes, I wrote a tribute to him after he died and it mentions angel wings."

I am relieved that she doesn't think I'm a little crazy. "He adds that he grew the wings, despite being a devil when he was here," I say, smiling. *This guy is really funny,* I think to myself. "You see, your brother had two sides to him. He was an enigma, secretive, when he was here. There was also a side to him that was transparent. He worked hard on trying to balance those when he was here and he's continuing that in spirit."

The reading now takes a more serious tone. "Around his passing, I feel much emotional turmoil and that he wasn't in a stable or good place when he crossed over. He wants you to know that he has now dealt with that in spirit. He wants you to pass this along to Mom and the person whose name starts with D-A."

I look at Cathy and notice that she seems a bit perplexed. "Ah, I don't know who that is." A moment later: "Oh, wait! We have a brother, David."

"He says David also tried to help him." The man infuses me with the familiar feeling of heaviness that I sense from spirits who have taken their own lives. "This passing comes through as very tragic. Is this a suicide?"

"Yes," Cathy confirms.

"Okay. It had that feel to it. He's really stressing that he got every bit of the healing and prayers you and the family sent to him after he passed. He says that the demon, his addiction, was smothering him. That's the hook he got caught on. He was okay for awhile here and then he relapsed."

After giving confirmation of older family members in spirit, I hear Cathy's brother say, *Tell her I'm sorry for what happened.* This message serves as a turning point in the reading and I notice that the line of communication becomes even stronger. The heavy brick wall begins to shatter. The man then impresses me with his personality: bright, creative, witty and artistic. He gives details about his life and recent events around his family. Cathy confirms several messages and agrees to check on the others.

Through clairsentience, I feel Cathy's brother put an emphasis on what I say next: "All of you did what you could do for him when he was here. That message applies very strongly to you and your husband. You also need to tell your mom to release her guilt around his death. He really wants to get that through. He emphasizes that there is nothing she did or didn't do that caused him to die. Please tell her that."

At this point, Cathy opens her eyes, as if she can finally see the truth concerning her brother's untimely death. Her bright blue eyes focus directly on me as I continue.

"He shows me a gun and I'm not sure why. Maybe he's trying to say that's how this happened? Your brother had an effervescent, charismatic personality at times. Then there was the other side to him. It feels bi-polar to me. Had he been diagnosed with that condition?"

"Yes, he had. No, he didn't use a gun to kill himself. He loved to hunt but I always tried to keep him away from guns because I was afraid he would hurt us with them."

I figure that the gun reference may be his way of showing details about his life. It made sense now how Cathy had tried to help her brother, who obviously had a difficult life. Although he didn't want to talk about the circumstances of how he took his life, this man wanted to make certain that his sister knew he went on in spirit. I look at the small clock on the table beside me; only a few minutes remain in the session. I ask the man for a final message. It comes in the form of feelings- gratitude and love- which I share with Cathy.

As we are saying goodbye, I extend my hand and tell Cathy to take good care of herself. Because I am still energetically tuned in, I observe that Cathy's energy field is far brighter than when she'd come in. The look on her face was softer and more relaxed than when she had arrived. As the reading revealed, she would undoubtedly be the anchor of healing for her family. I have no doubt that Cathy, her brother and their family have begun to lift the veil of pain that initially separated them in the aftermath of his untimely death. Another level of healing had begun for all of them.

The Reunited Family

Not long ago, I did a session with two sisters in which spirit communication set the stage for forgiveness. As you will see, their father relayed the BP about his life and how it affected the lives of his children in terms of negative family patterns. It's an impressive example of how toxic emotions are carried from generation to generation until they are released. During the session, Allie and Becky also inform me that they believe their mother in spirit has been instrumental in bringing the family back together after years of a rift.

"The first energy I'm aware of is the older male," I begin. "He says he's someone's dad."

Allie is the first to speak up. "He's our father."

This spirit immediately begins to give me information. "Do the two of you have a different mother?" I ask. "Did someone marry twice in the family?"

"Well, I did," Allie responds. "Or do you mean someone on

the other side?"

"Yes."

"Our father married twice."

"I thought so because he's giving me the impression of two different families being connected to you. He shows me a split in the two families."

Both women nod.

"Your mother is here, as well. She is with him. His second marriage would have been after he was married to your mom, right?"

"Yes," Allie confirms.

"Even though they didn't stay together in life, they are coming through here as a unit. Now the name John is being mentioned."

"That's our brother," both women say in unison.

"Tell him they came through and acknowledge him. They also mention another name that starts with J-O."

"Our sister, Joanne," Becky says.

"Mentioning them is your parents' way of including them in the reading. Here are some identifying factors: Someone passed from a heart or lung problem and someone makes me feel the solar plexus area of the body was affected with illness."

"Our dad died from a heart attack. Mom had ovarian cancer."

A number of detailed messages about the parents follow before this message comes through for Allie: "Your mom wants you to know that through difficult times in your life, she's been there. She says that you've undergone many circumstances in your life that have led to a tremendous change in you. Some of them have been quite painful. She emphasizes that she's been with you through all of that."

"Uh-huh," Allie says quietly. I sense she knows exactly what her mom is referring to.

"There are two ways she'll come through to you: by your intuition, which gives you the correct path to follow, and through hugs from her. People here are giving you hugs and you are reaching out more to others. She wants you to know that she's included in that embrace, as well."

"Okay," Allie says, smiling. Becky sits wide-eyed as the communication flows.

"Your mom tells me that there's been a big transition with a relationship—moving out of one, that is."

Allie nods.

"She makes me feel as if this situation was abusive for you. You're the snake that's shed its skin or the butterfly emerging from its chrysalis. In fact, she's sent you butterflies as a sign of her presence and hope. The wings are symbolic of you spreading your wings, flying a different direction, transformation and rising above problems. She says you're in a much better space now emotionally."

Several other messages about Allie's past relationship come through, which the sisters validate. Soon after, I get a sense that Allie has been emotionally distraught. To validate this, I ask: "Did you at one point not want to be here anymore?"

"Yes," Allie responds.

"Did you actually have a suicide attempt?"

"Yes."

"Your mom shows me that she cradled you, as only a mother can, during those really rough times. You were meant to be here and you have a purpose here. She's reflected a lot of that to you," I say to Allie, referring to her sister, Becky. "Your mom has come through her. Pay close attention to what Becky says."

The two women look at one another and laugh. "Just the other day I said to Becky that she sounds like Mom!" Allie comments. "Whew!"

At this point, I feel a shift in who is communicating with us from the spirit world. "Someone was involved in the military."

"Oh, I think that's our Uncle Bill, dad's brother."

"You're going to hear from your dad now. His side is coming through," I say as I tune in to hear more. "Your mom steps back and your dad is communicating. He claims some sort of responsibility in the way he related to both of you, especially emotionally. He wants to wipe the slate clean—not to excuse what he did but to allow healing to begin. You've already talked about some of these issues—self-esteem, self-worth—in counseling. He's well aware of how his behavior affected the family. Now you know that you don't have to carry all of this anymore."

Allie and Becky are engrossed in every word their father is delivering. "This also frees him up to continue on the other side," I explain. "He says your brother has also had some problems with self-esteem in his life."

"Yeah, he has," Allie answers.

"Your dad wants you to be happier than he was when he was here. I'm not sure you would have heard that from him when he *was* here."

Becky shakes her head in agreement.

"Nor did he understand as much as he does now. He wants you to release the past and move forward. He mentions the name Rich."

"My ex-husband," Becky confirms.

"He refers to him in regard to what was just communicated about relationships. That marriage was a difficult relationship for you. You know, your adult relationships have been affected by the one you had with your dad. He shows himself as a less than admirable role model."

"Yes," Becky concurs.

"He refers to a name starting with C-H, like Charlie."

"My ex-husband," Allie chimes in. "I guess he's bringing it up as another example of domestic abuse."

"He encourages you to find happiness and to not remain stuck in family patterns that were set up years ago. This is a time of transformation for both of you. You can't afford to be immersed in the pain and drama anymore."

"I know," Allie says with conviction.

"You have to establish a link with a higher power so that you don't get swept away in the chaos." I feel the energy from the other side shift. "Okay, your mom and dad are pulling back now. They've been very direct here, but also very loving. They balance those two qualities. It used to be called 'tough love', I believe. Your parents will inspire you through your intuition."

"Can you ask Mom if I'm on the right track in life?" Becky asks before the link is broken.

"She doesn't comment on your work but she makes me feel that she wants you to do what fulfills you. If something isn't working for you, get out. You have often tried to carry others' burdens, especially in relationships. You know, it's called being the martyr. I hate to make it sound so harsh but that's the way she's bringing it through."

Becky smiles knowingly. I sense she understands that what her mother is saying is the truth.

After the session ends, we chat about how the reading validated the difficult relationship that the sisters shared with their father and the loving perspective of their mother. Becky comments that she believes her mom was working behind the scenes, from the spirit world, to reunite the two sisters after a long-time separation. We also discuss how they've been alerted by their parents to change the old family patterns regarding toxic relationships.

"The validations that Dad gave will help me heal and move forward with my life," Allie concludes.

Before the women leave, I remind them that they need to replenish the energy they'd lost to painful relationships through self-love and forgiveness. The promising light of awareness had begun to illuminate the tunnel of darkness they and their family had been trapped in for so long, thanks to their willingness to receive it.

Six

Would-Haves, Should-Haves, Could-Haves

The wound is the place where the Light enters you.
Rumi

An all-too-common emotion that people struggle with after losing a loved one is guilt, the basis of which often concerns the timing and circumstances of death or relationship regrets that now seem "unfixable." People question what would have happened if only they could've had more time with or expressed more love to deceased loved ones, if medical treatment would have been different than it was or if the outcome of an illness would have been discovered earlier. I have also read for those who are continually tortured by prior decisions they made while responsible for a loved one's care.

Guilt is self-destructive because it prevents us from making closure with death, moving on in life and finding peace. Much like walking on an endless treadmill that leads nowhere, it imprisons our minds in a past that no longer exists and cannot be changed, except by our willingness to forgive. Eventually, guilt can lead to depression, self-loathing and, worst of all, hopelessness. The seed from which guilt sprouts is the illusion that we possess the ultimate control over another's life and death—when, in reality, we do not. I am referring to the spiritual truth that everything (death included) happens in accordance with divine order, despite outward appearances that may indicate otherwise. Coupled with the illusion of control is the self-created expectation we impose on how and when death should happen; then we go on to harbor guilt over the part we think we *should* have played when these personal expectations are not realized.

The transcripts in this chapter focus on how guilt can be transformed through wisdom that is infinitely higher than our own ego. These sessions are representative of many I have done in which people confront their self-imposed expectations regarding a loved one's death.

No More Guilt Trips

The following client first contacted me after reading my book, *I'm Still with You*. I am choosing to share Laura's story because it's a classic example of how individuals carry unresolved guilt about death and how spirit loved ones are aware of family members' emotional states.

"Hi Carole," Laura says in greeting. "Would you mind explaining how this works? I've never had a consult with a medium before. Psychics, yes, but not a medium."

Even though Laura is many miles away, I feel her nervousness. "Sure, Laura. I'll say my prayer then I'll ask what you want me to focus on. There are many things that can be discussed in readings. It's best to be open. I will interpret what I am sensing around you and . . ."

"But . . ." Laura interrupts, ". . . how do we make the connection over the phone?"

"Because I am reading energy, it doesn't matter what distance is between us. That's irrelevant. Your voice transmits energy and the spirit world is energy. It's like prayer; that's a good analogy to help you understand."

Laura seems satisfied with this explanation, so I begin. "There's someone here who is a father-like energy, either your dad or your father-in-law. There's a connection to someone who passed from a cardiovascular issue and someone who had strokes. Also, do you know who would have had dementia? A woman comes through with that identification."

Laura pauses to consider all of this information. "That could be my father. I knew my grandmother, his mother, but I don't know how she died."

"Okay, well, you may have to research that to find out, but that is what I feel."

"Oh, wait! I believe my mother had a stroke before she passed."

"Alright," I say quickly, aware that another spirit wants to come through. "Someone just said 'Jim.' Do you know who that is, please?"

"Yes! That's my late husband's brother, who is still alive."

"Usually, when the name of someone living is mentioned, it's a reference to a health condition with that person. I'm sensing this is true in Jim's case."

"He's okay, but he's had serious heart problems in the past."

"Okay. Your husband is here and he says he's visited with you or another family member before this reading through a dream. He makes reference to passing from cancer, either stomach or pancreatic."

"Oh, my God!" Laura gasps. "That's exactly where his cancer was!"

"Yes, he was very ill. There was a lot of pain going on with him. This message is kind of humorous, but he wants to let you know that he can eat again."

Laura again exclaims, "Oh, my God!" "He loved to eat before he got sick!"

The next message comes through with gusto: "He says there was not a chance of him beating the illness, Laura. He makes me feel that things were too far gone and it wasn't really an option for him to stay in the physical realm. You know that, right?"

"Yes," Laura says, her voice breaking up. "Can I say something?"

"Yes, of course."

"I feel so guilty because I couldn't save him!" Now Laura is sobbing full out.

"Dear, you have to let go of carrying that guilt now. That's why he is bringing through this message about the illness being too advanced for his life to be saved. Do you understand? You've carried guilt ever since his passing. It's time to let it go."

"I can't! I took care of him forever in so many other ways, and he was never sick. I don't know how I couldn't have seen that happening. I blame myself."

"You need to stop blaming yourself. I feel as if you have been getting messages intuitively around that issue. Spirit, the divine life force, is moving now to help you step out of self-depreciating, heavy emotions about your husband's death. Part of the purpose of this reading today is for your husband to say what *wasn't* said before he died. Part of that is the message for you to let go of the guilt because you couldn't save him."

Laura regains her composure and listens silently.

"He is making me feel that there was a misdiagnosis of his illness or that some symptoms were ignored or misunderstood by him or his doctors. You had nothing to do with that. It was just the way things unfolded. Let me explain. There is a divine timing connected with our souls. Even though it may not make sense to us logically, there is timing as to when the soul makes a transition back to the spirit world. What we expect should have been different is often beyond our control. Understanding that means we don't have to carry guilt. Please take that into your heart and consider it."

I perceive that this message hits home with Laura. "Once you really get all of this, you will be free to move on. When you begin to think, 'If only the tumors would have been discovered sooner,' call upon Spirit to help you release that guilt."

"Did he know how sick he was?"

"Yes. It was difficult for him to be sick. It was hard for him to ask for help with the simplest things such as eating and using the bathroom. You were down there in the trenches with him, helping him through this."

"Does he know how much I love him?" Laura asks, her voice filled with emotion.

"You tell him that all the time." I respond.

"I do! Every day, I do. Does he really hear me?"

"Yes! He says that you talk to him. There's a photo of him in the bedroom that you talk to."

"That's true!"

"He says that you need to start enjoying yourself more with travel. Wasn't there an invitation regarding travel that came to you in the last several months that you turned down?"

"Well, yes, there was. It was a trip to Las Vegas with our friends."

"Okay, he wants you to go. It's going to come up again for you to go. Give yourself permission to enjoy life."

"Okay," Laura says flatly.

She doesn't get the message. "It's okay to enjoy yourself again. He shows me that an opportunity to travel will come again in October. Just take the money and do it."

I stay in the zone to see what final messages might filter through. "Michael is being acknowledged."

"He's our very best friend. Oh, my God! He just had surgery yesterday."

"Your husband says, 'Send him my best.' Now I get the feeling that there is a significant date—a birthday or death—around this time."

"My husband's passing was this month."

"There's a strong emphasis here that instead of being sad about his death, celebrate his life, your marriage and your family. You can then start to turn your emotions around. You could say, 'I'm really grateful for the time we had.' That's what he wants."

Laura's husband delivers two powerful evidential messages before the end of the reading: "Hello to Robert. He also sends me a clairvoyant image of a car. Do you know what that means? It's definitely connected to your family."

"Robert is another good friend. I'll tell him. Our daughter has his car."

"There was some minor repair recently done to it."

"Hmm, I'm not sure. I'll check with my daughter."

As the reading concludes, I remind Laura to release the restrictive emotions she is carrying and open herself to the possibility of finding love again. "Your husband says he'll bring someone, a companion, into your life. He encourages you to be open to having a new relationship."

A minute or so before I end the reading, I suddenly get the impression of another spirit coming through. "Hold on. There's someone here who had beautiful flower gardens, a name starting with an 'H.' She wants to let you know she is here."

"My mother, Helen. She was known for her flower gardens. I've always felt she was with my husband after he passed. My parents were very close to him. That's nice to know. Thank you."

Immediately after the session, I feel that a significant shift has taken place in Laura's emotions. Her late husband came through and helped her to wipe the slate clean of the heavy guilt she'd been carrying for months, possibly years. Although I have not yet received feedback from her, I am certain that Laura's life took a turn for the better that day, thanks to her husband's undying love.

Dad Shows the BP

When elderly parents require advanced care and medical treatment that family members are not capable of providing, it often necessitates moving them to an assisted living or long-term care facility. Despite the obvious benefits to individuals receiving this type of care, their children may harbor guilt over making the decision to move them, especially if parents resist what is actually for their own good. Unfortunately, the painful feelings of anger and guilt that can result from these situations are the last memories that children have of a once loving relationship.

The following two sessions exemplify how hearing from parents in spirit helps their adult children move beyond guilt. In the first, a father shares his expanded vision about difficult decisions made by his daughter prior to his passing. The second story chronicles a guilt-ridden daughter who hears from her mother after she passes from the debilitating effects of Alzheimer's disease.

As I say my prayer to open the first session, I feel Spirit impress me in my abdomen. I sense this indicates a physical issue with either Judy, my client, or her loved one in spirit. I ask Judy if she has health concerns in that area of her body.

"I do," she says, "but it could also be someone in spirit."

"The feeling is that someone had a stomach tumor."

"Yes, that's right! It's the person I want to hear from today."

"Let's start with that," I continue. "It was cancer that spread in the abdominal region. I'm aware of an older male energy connected to you, a father or uncle."

"Yes, it's my father that I want to connect with. He had colon cancer and it spread to his liver."

A few minutes pass in which I give identification of other relatives who come through with Judy's father, then the communication with him resumes.

"Your dad says he had a long illness and that he is glad to be over that. There were periods of time when he felt well and went into remission before he got really ill. He acknowledges you as a primary caretaker and that it is now necessary for you to take care of yourself because of your own health issues. Please keep up with the routine procedures he says you've had in the past, especially since cancer runs in your family."

"Ah, yes. I've had a colonoscopy, but that was five years ago. I guess he's reminding me that it's time to have another one."

"Your dad shows me that he lost weight and his digestion was badly affected by the illness. He doesn't want that to happen to you."

Judy's dad was certainly on the ball about giving his daughter health information for her own good. I smile inwardly, as I am beginning to feel as if I work in a doctor's office or hospital. Although I do not want to control the reading, I silently ask him to give other types of messages. After a few more health-related messages, he switches to another topic.

"Who [alive] has had dreams about your dad? He says that he's come through in that way."

"My mother has, but they have not been good ones," Judy confirms.

"Hmm . . . he wants to add that he's heard you when you talk to him and that he gives you inspirational advice."

"I knew it was him. I'll feel really low and then after talking to him, I feel better."

"You get keyed up, anxious about things; on the other hand, you can get very down. He makes me feel these two extremes with you. It'll become increasingly important for you to modulate those feelings."

"Well, it's been difficult lately. I've had added responsibility with my mom, their dogs, selling their house and other things."

Judy's dad gives me a feeling that he wants to talk about the care of his wife, Judy's mother. Again, I feel sensations in my body. "She has dementia and problems with her hips and legs. He says there was a move involved with mom's caretaking."

"She's now in a nursing facility," Judy sighs. "She fell and broke her hip before my dad passed."

"He comes around her. Your mom is not the easiest person to take of. There's much that requires tending to with her. You don't have to feel as if you are copping out on a responsibility by keeping her in the care facility. He says that it's the best decision you could have made," I relay with emphasis.

Upon hearing this, Judy starts to cry. "Oh, I'm so glad to hear that!"

"He's really stressing that message because of your guilt.

Remember the earlier message about taking care of yourself? You've done so much caretaking of others; now you must return that to yourself."

"That was one of the questions I had for him today," Judy says, choking up. "I wanted to see if he approved of mom being in a facility."

"That's why he brought that message through," I confirm. "There are repetitive thoughts you have, like 'should I have done this or that?' He's saying that everything has unfolded exactly as it needs to be. He gives me a feeling that there was so much on your plate. You did what you felt was necessary and it's okay."

"He was upset that I had to move him to the same facility my mom is in. I just couldn't handle taking care of both of them at the same time. I've felt guilt over having to move them."

"Well, he's not upset now. When we get to the other side, we go back into a pure spiritual state. We are able to see the Big Picture. Even though your dad may have been cantankerous about being moved, he now understands why you did what you did. Release the guilt around this. You know, the guilt you're carrying is a factor in the stomach discomfort you have."

"Right," Judy answers in a subdued voice.

"You can write about your feelings, do prayers for self-forgiveness, meditate, go to counseling or talk to friends. These are all ways to work through negative emotions."

"It means so much to have him say these things."

"Your dad says he will be there for your mom when it's her time to cross over. By the way, there's an acknowledgment for James."

"That's my husband. He's a doctor and he also took care of my dad."

Suddenly it makes sense why Judy's dad had come through with so many messages of a medical nature. Being married to a doctor would obviously make Judy familiar with healthcare. As the reading progresses, Judy wants to know if her father had been giving her signs that he was around. Again, I am impressed with medical information—specifically, an image of a reddening in the eye area. I share this with Judy.

"My mom is always complaining that her eyes are red and inflamed. Is he saying that he's around her and she knows this?"

"Yes, that's exactly what he's saying. Sorry to back up here, but your dad wants to make sure you get his apology. He didn't mean to be so difficult when he was here; he says he didn't feel well."

"We know that," Judy replies. "After he passed, I said to him, 'Well, now you can see the big picture."

I laugh because of the obvious synchronicity of Judy's words with mine. "Please know he is there for you and your mom. Oh, the name Betty is being mentioned."

"That's Mom's name!" Judy exclaims. "Mom says that she feels him around her and it unnerves her."

"He stresses that he's there to help her, not scare her. Does your mom believe in mediumship? Could you share with her that your dad is around her and will be waiting to reunite with her when she crosses over?"

"Yes, she believes in this. She's lost a lot: her husband, her house and her beloved dogs. Her world has been totally turned upside down."

"Yes, she's in transition and that's difficult. Your father is helping her with this and says to tell her she's not alone. She is like a frightened child. I sense a lot of fear with her."

"She has been like that her whole life. She has always been afraid of losing *something*. Is her death in the foreseeable future?" Judy inquires.

"I'm not being shown that here. But I *can* tell you that your dad is present for her. It's hard for people to understand sometimes, but those in spirit are as close to us as our breath."

"I understand, I think. I do need to tell my mom that she is not alone because she has felt as if I've dumped her in a nursing home. She doesn't realize how much care she requires."

"Your dad is making me feel that the physical wear and tear on you would be terrible. Hold on, there's a name being mentioned: Eileen. Who is that?"

"She's my mom's roommate at the nursing home!"

"That's amazing," I say. "That's your dad's way of letting you know he is definitely around your mom there."

Before the reading concludes, I ask Judy if she has any questions, and she asks the million dollar one.

"What is my purpose in life? I feel as if I might have missed it since I've done so much caretaking of others."

"You are a member of the soul group of caretakers," I respond. "In the eyes of Spirit, this is just as important and valid as being the President of the United States, for example. It may seem as if it would not be, but it is. Your soul has agreed to learn compassion, patience and unconditional love in this way. In conclusion, I want you to know all of this has been your dad's way of coming through to you today."

Before we part, Judy says, "I feel so much better. I'm so thankful that my dad came through and told me to release the guilt." I feel blessed to have been the conduit to connect father with daughter, especially since the reading would help Judy with the care of her mother. In the days ahead, she would have the assurance that she was indeed meeting her purpose, unrestrained by guilt.

I'm Happy You are Free, Mom

Caring for someone who has Alzheimer's disease can be extremely challenging for families and other loved ones. As the condition progresses over the years, those who are afflicted often become emotionally detached from family and friends; they can undergo dramatic changes in personality and become oblivious to their physical surroundings. It is especially heartbreaking for loved ones when these memories are the last ones they have of a once vibrant, loving person. As you will see in the following session, this condition is healed once souls return to the spirit world. This story demonstrates how a mother's love transcends death and helps transform her surviving daughter's guilt into acceptance.

"Someone had an extended illness," I begin as I tune in to read for Gina on the other end of the phone.

"My mother did," she responds.

"She says that she was in bed for a long time and she points to her legs, where there was a problem. She is with a contemporary male energy who preceded her into spirit, your dad or uncle."

"That would be my uncle, her brother. She was totally unable to walk due to Alzheimer's."

In my mind's eye, I see a woman rapidly twirling around with her arms moving back and forth. "This is interesting. I see your mother dancing on the other side. That is her way of saying that she is free from all physical problems. She says that when she was here, she felt like a prisoner in her body, although she learned many spiritual lessons from going through that long illness."

"That's wonderful to hear."

"Your mom has spent time in a place on the other side, a resting place, a hospital of sorts. This is common with people who have had long illnesses prior to passing. She talks about a move. Did you have to move her into a care facility?" I ask.

"Well, we had to move her from her home several states away so that she could be closer to me."

"She makes me feel that it was hard for her to lose capacity. She had much emotion attached to that, but she doesn't want you or your dad to hold any bad feelings about that. Both of you are still processing how you feel about decisions that had to be made in her best interest. She can see now that things had to be done in the way they were. This feels like a very significant message for you."

A moment of silence passes then Gina speaks: "It's right on. My dad became ill and he could no longer care for her. That's why we moved her. But because of my other duties, like work and family, I've felt guilty about placing her in a care facility."

"She gives me a strong feeling that you need not hold that anymore. She did not grasp that at the time. She was resistant and may have said, 'Why can't I stay with you?' That sparked many feelings of guilt within you. Now she can see why things were as they were. She wants to tell you that she has already come to you inspirationally, urging you to get rid of the guilt. Now you are hearing that message verbally."

"Yes, thank you," Gina says softly.

"Your mom has transformed from the incapacitated, frail individual who you watched decline into the beautiful soul that she actually is. She was very excited to show you that today. This is how she wants you to remember her. Your mom makes me feel that she had a full, productive life before her illness. There's a big deal here with her being in the kitchen. Also, she shows me some sort of potato dish or salad. I'm not sure what that means."

"That's funny! She had a famous mashed potato recipe that she brought to all our family functions. It was our family's favorite. You're dead-on," Gina confirms.

"She put much love into her cooking. She says that there is a family gathering that is either coming or just passed in which her recipes were made or mentioned."

"Yes! My father just celebrated his 90th birthday last weekend. We all got together and toasted Mom, the only one not there."

"She *was* there with you. I am hearing about a family member whose name begins with the letters A-L. Do you know who that is?"

"Alex, her grandson."

"She shows me that he is going back to school."

"That's amazing! He wants to go back to school, but he has a good job that he's not sure he wants to give up. He is in turmoil about going back to get his PhD."

"Your mom sends her regards to him and to all of you. She was very much a family-oriented person. She wants me to tell you that your dad will be okay without her."

"Sometimes he wonders why he's still here, but I know he will be until his lessons are completed," Gina says.

"Yes. Sometimes we don't know what those are until we cross over because they are beyond our comprehension. Your father is doing well for his age."

"Yes, he is."

"Your mom gives references to her hair, nails and make-up related to how you cared for her. You need to know that taking care of those things for her made her feel comfortable."

"Oh, yes! I took her to the beauty parlor in the nursing home and put on her make-up everyday."

"To her, this mattered. She's letting you know that showed love and caring for her."

"I wonder, given her state of mind, if she really knew what was going on."

"Obviously, she did since she is mentioning it now. What I've seen through my work is that with a condition like Alzheimer's, the person is in and out of the body a lot. Individuals with this illness actually spend time on the other side."

"Oh, really?"

"Yes. When we try to connect with a living person who has this condition, sometimes they're not really there mentally because the consciousness spends time on the astral plane, the spirit world. Your mom is making me feel this is what she did, although she was also aware of what was happening here. She says you gave her back rubs, as well."

"Yes, I did!"

"The name Estelle is being mentioned."

"That's my mom's sister-in-law who passed before her."

"She is with her on the other side. I'm to let you know that your mom comes to you through scent, particularly a perfume that was hers."

"I know what she means," Gina replies. "I have her perfume and when I use it, I think of her."

"I am hearing a name that begins with S-H or C-H that means something to you."

"My son, Charlie! Does she have any advice for him? She was very close to him."

I wait for more information. "It concerns your son having difficulty in school. Would that be an attention deficit problem?"

"Yes. He had many problems when he was younger. I hope he is now overcoming those."

"She shows much achievement around your son in the business world. She also shows me a new car."

"Well, my daughter is looking at one now! It's astounding to me that people in spirit are so in tune with our everyday lives—what food we prepare, getting a new car—that just amazes me!"

"The reason is to let you know that their consciousness goes on. After death, we are still alive. We do go on yet we are aware of our family's lives, too."

"Did Mom know how sick she was when she was here?"

"In my experience, when theses souls pass, the mental condition such as Alzheimer's is left behind. In between living and dying, there is time spent on the other side, where the person can see what is happening with the physical body. They are shown that their time isn't finished yet and they must go back into the body. When your mom passed, it wasn't that difficult of an adjustment since she had already spent time there."

As the session draws to a close, Gina's mom continues to impress me with details of her life. "Your mom shows me embroidery."

"Yes. We have pieces of those scattered around my dad's house. She was very good at embroidery. Before time runs out in the session, I want to ask about something. In the last few years, my purpose was to be a caretaker. Now I feel lost. I guess I'm trying to figure out what to do now."

"No matter what you choose to do, you're meeting purpose because you are being Spirit. The secondary purpose is 'doing' Spirit in the outside world. My sense is that you will teach others about what you have gone through. You'll also pass knowledge along in your work and through volunteering."

Before the reading ends, Gina's mom gives one last, powerful message: "She was very happy to be out of her body; shedding it was like coming out of a butterfly's chrysalis. You will get messages from her through the symbol of a butterfly."

"I already have," Gina announces. "A friend sent me a greeting card with a butterfly on it not long after Mom passed. We had often talked about how death is a transformation, like the butterfly. The last few months of her life were horrible. She couldn't eat or hold her head up. I kept praying for God to let her go. I hope she knows how much I love her."

"She wants me to assure you she knows," I tell her.

A few months ago, I did another session for Gina, during which her father- who had passed since our first reading- came through and told her he was reunited with her mom in spirit. At the time, I perceived a positive change in Gina's emotions from our earlier session. The guilt she had carried was replaced by reassurance in knowing that she had done the best she could for both parents. Some time later, she mailed me a card in which she expressed gratitude for the readings that had helped her cope with the loss of her parents. Little did she know that I had been in need of receiving just such a boost to re-invigorate my commitment to my work. Her words reawakened me to the real healing potential that spirit communication offers. For a few weeks, I displayed the card on my dining room table as a "testimonial" that my work was making a difference for people. I gave thanks for my abilities as a medium.

The New House by the Lake

I frequently help people confront emotional blockages that they may have carried for years. In most of these cases, individuals allow their past experiences, beliefs and painful mindsets to control them to the extent that they close themselves off to any prospect of living a productive, happy life. One of the most difficult circumstances that people have to cope with involves estrangement from a loved one prior to their death. The next session is with a woman who was consumed with guilt over the last words she had with her husband.

At the beginning of the reading, several spirits quickly connect with me. I give the evidence as quickly as I can. "An older male energy is coming in here, your father or uncle. A contemporary male energy is also here, a spouse, brother or cousin. He is stepping forward and saying, 'I'm the one she wants to hear from.' There's another father-like energy here, as well. Have you lost a father-in-law, too?"

"Yes," Debbie verifies, "but my husband did not really have a relationship with him."

"That doesn't matter. Your husband is showing you that he has a relationship with him now in spirit. Someone has lost a brother, as well."

"My husband's brother just passed away three months ago."

I quickly realize that Debbie's husband- the person she wants to hear from- is focused on bringing through substantial evidence to identify himself. I sensed there was a lot more to come from him. *This is good. Now let's get to the meat of the reading.* I silently ask him to talk about any unfinished emotional business. "He says his father went away at a young age. There was an emotional disconnect between them. Who drank too much?"

"His dad!"

"He wants me to tell you that since he has passed, he's made peace with their relationship. That affected him deeply. Your marriage provided love that wasn't present for him as a child. His dad was very self-absorbed. His mom is with him on the other side, too. Also, someone had heart problems prior to passing."

"We found out [through an autopsy] after my husband passed that he had coronary artery disease."

I explain to Debbie that her other relatives and in-laws sense her grief and are coming through to show their support. "Your husband says he comes around you at night and that you have had problems sleeping."

"Yes, I have. It's because he's gone. I do feel him at night. I have reading lights and sometimes they will flicker."

"He's letting you know that he is right beside you. He knows how hard it's been for you to go on. Consider yourself blessed that you are getting these signs because many people don't. He says you've checked the bulbs on these lights and couldn't find anything wrong."

"Yes, I have checked them!"

"Who is Robert?"

"That's my husband!" Debbie exclaims loudly, her voice filled with emotion.

"You need to know that he also comes to you through feelings. Please understand that this is not like the person being there with you physically; it is more subtle. A feeling that he wants me to give you now is comfort. He wants you to know that he is okay and that you need to continue with your life. You've thought, 'I don't want to be here anymore,' haven't you?"

On the other end of the phone, I hear Debbie sob. "Yes. He hasn't been gone that long. It's true. I don't want to be here anymore. I don't!" she says emphatically.

"I know, but you *are* here. Your heart is still immersed in grief and you must allow the feelings to come up. Make a spiritual connection, whatever that is for you. When it is time for you to go into the spirit world, he says he'll be there for you. But right now you are still here and you have a life to live. The connection will always be there."

An image of a large, serene lake forms in my mind. As usual, I have no idea what this image means to Debbie so I describe it to her.

"I'm moving to a new house by a lake soon," she confirms.

"I see. He says you'll be taking him with you. I sense that means his remains."

Debbie laughs softly. "I have his urn on the bookshelf and I'll definitely be taking him with me."

"He's a good communicator and has a beautiful smile. He was a self-made man and an entrepreneur."

"That's exactly what he was. Why haven't I been able to hear him?" Debbie seems a bit frustrated.

"You must understand that grief is a heavy energy. There are different vibrations to emotions; for example, joy and gratitude are light; sadness, anger and jealousy are dense, just like grief. These prevent you from hearing Spirit. That's another reason why he sends you physical signals, like flickering lights."

Another clairvoyant image enters my mind. "He shows me a candle that is somehow connected to him. What does that mean to you?"

"Every night I light two candles for him on my bed stand. His photo is next to them."

"He says you're buying new furniture, specifically new cabinets."

"I'm doing that right now! I just ordered new cabinets."

As the reading winds down, I ask Debbie if she has questions.

"Does he say how he passed?"

I tune in. "There seems to be a question mark around that. You're still not at peace with that."

"I still wonder about it. Ask him if he considers me the cause of his death."

I think this is a curious question, but I remind myself that nothing I hear from people in the living or the other side really surprises me anymore. "Hmm . . . he makes me feel there was a problem in some part of his body and the severity of that was not realized at the time. That's about all he wants to say about that."

Debbie sighs. "Okay, here is why I ask. We had an argument and our last words to each other were not the nicest ones, especially after 26 years together. He had a habit of leaving when he got angry at me. His last words that day were, 'If you follow me, I'll file for divorce.' The next day, when I didn't hear from him, I drove to where he was and I found his body."

I could feel how devastating this had been for Debbie. "This was a very quick passing. He had undiagnosed cardiac problems and high blood pressure."

"But does he say anything else that would have been involved?" Debbie is insistent so I tune inward for further information that could help.

"Well, he says there was some sort of drug or medication involved."

"Yes, there was and . . . "

I interrupt Debbie before she discloses anything that might come through. "Hold on . . . you need to know that the argument you had with him did not cause his death. Do you still carry guilt over this?"

"Yes, I still carry it," Debbie cries.

"He does not give me the feeling that you caused his passing," I say emphatically.

"He was taking sleeping pills and I never found a bottle of them after his death. I thought he might have committed suicide but the coroner said he didn't; he had advanced coronary artery disease, just as you are saying now."

"I don't know what good it will serve you to go over and over what happened. My feeling is that a combination of factors caused his death. Yes, the pills may have contributed, but the message here concerns your release of guilt."

"He could have had so much more in life. He was only 50. I feel as if I didn't have enough time with him. I don't understand."

"There is a divine timing with each soul. This may not make sense to our logical mind but when we cross over, we understand. As with the rest of the natural world, there is a time for everything, including death. There is perfection to our souls, including when and how we pass. Healing involves acceptance, and acceptance means the end of suffering. I recommend that you ask Spirit to bring you into acceptance by letting go of needing to know *why* and *how*. It's interesting that he didn't come through with a reference to the argument you had. I sense that is because it's water over the dam, as far as he is concerned. It's already forgiven."

"I forgive him but I still feel guilty."

"Have you gone to counseling?"

"I did. I wanted to take my own life to be with him, but I discovered that if I did that, I wouldn't be with him. I mean, suicides go to different places over there, don't they? At least that's what I've heard. So I decided to move into a new house, to make a new life for myself."

I decide to not address the suicide question because it would detract from the communication with her husband. I don't want to lose the link with him. "Good for you. By the way, he adds that you've written him letters."

"I write to him all the time."

"Good. That is a form of release. Much of your life energy is in the past. In order to heal, you must pull it into the present, instead of going over and over about what happened. This gives you the incredible power available in the moment."

The reading draws to an end. I offer Debbie reassurance that she is indeed moving forward, away from the burdens of grief and guilt. In addition to her husband coming through with substantial evidence about himself and their life together, the reading revealed to her that the spiritual power residing within her is strong enough to liberate her from the prison of the past.

Although she still has a way to go, Debbie now has every reason to live.

Seven

Toxic Emotions

Most folks are about as happy as they make up their minds to be.
Abraham Lincoln

From as far back as I can remember, I've allowed my emotions to strongly influence me. As a child, I was thin-skinned-emotionally fragile and painfully impressionable. Before I recognized my abilities as a medium, I did not understand why I was extremely sensitive to people and events, both around me and in the world. I had no idea how to disengage from my internal, gut-level reactions and the outside circumstances that triggered them. In those early days, I certainly didn't understand that I could use this sensitivity in a positive way to help others.

By my teen years, I'd discovered that drugs and alcohol were potent anesthetics to squelch the gnawing pain of feeling too much. A decade later, in the throes of addiction, I found myself at the end of my rope—physically, mentally, emotionally and spiritually. It was not until I began to attend 12-step programs that I learned I no longer had to be a victim of my own emotions. I came to understand that life was not going to change on the outside; rather, I had to identify and temper my knee-jerk reactions to it by changing myself on the inside. During that dark, low point, I realized that the quality of my life depended on my willingness to let go of what wasn't working for me. For years, I had allowed my ego and feelings to take center stage in my life. Through recovery, I became aware of another dimension that extended far beyond feeling. The 12-step groups that I attended called it a Higher Power.

It was not until years later, through my practice of

mediumship, that I understood through that same Higher Power how much of an impact my own struggles with emotions could have on helping others. In all the years I've been doing readings, I cannot recall a single session in which a client's emotions were not discussed in some way. Whether life concerns or contact with deceased loved ones are involved, feelings always come up. As the case studies throughout this book indicate, I frequently sit with people who have unresolved emotions such as anger, grief, fear, restlessness and resentment concerning loved ones in spirit or the circumstances of their death. If held for long periods of time, these emotions become toxins that poison and harden the heart and mind. When this happens, there is little chance of experiencing closure and peace—at least until these toxins are released through a spiritual intervention, an awareness of oneself that extends beyond feeling and mind.

In many readings, souls will come through and address unresolved emotions and lingering relationship issues that existed at the time of their death. With the help of my spirit guides, guidance to move beyond this "stop gap" is offered. Resolution can then begin for everyone involved.

The sessions in this chapter are representative of many I have done in which those on the other side bring their spiritual light to surviving family members who are not at peace, for one reason or another. As you read these stories, my hope is that you will be inspired to detoxify your own unresolved emotions by opening your heart and releasing them to Spirit. It makes no difference whatsoever how long you have suffered; the opportunity to begin fresh is now.

The Soul Mate Connection

Diana's voice, coming over the phone from Europe, carries the heavy weight of grief. She seems taken aback when I greet her warmly, as if annoyed by my upbeat mood. Wanting to keep the energy high for the reading, I ask her in a pleasant tone what she wants me to focus on in the session.

"I need closure with my husband," she announces abruptly. "I'd also like to know if I have angels and guides around me."

I close my eyes to focus inward. "The first energy I'm aware of is a father. This must be your husband's dad."

"Yes."

"There's another man with him also, a contemporary to his dad. This is probably your husband's uncle."

"Oh, yes. He loved his uncle very much. He was named after him- Ed."

"They're making me feel as if that answers a question for you. You wanted to know who your husband is with, didn't you?"

"Yes. I've wondered about that."

With three spirits coming through at once, it's impossible for me to separate one's thoughts from another's; however, I feel strongly that they want to communicate their closeness to one another—both in life and on the other side. "All three impress me with being upstanding and loyal to the family. I also feel that someone here has passed from cancer."

"All three did," Diana responds.

"Your husband had quite a struggle with his illness. He says that you were with him throughout the journey. The lack of closure you are now feeling is emotional. You are grieving the loss of his physical presence. Have you felt him around you?"

"Nothing I can be definite about," she says in a rigid tone.

"He says that he comes around, particularly at night."

"Oh, since I made the appointment to talk with you, I had a dream about him, but it wasn't a nice feeling. It was uncomfortable. It didn't feel like a reunion."

"Was it fear-based?" I ask.

"Yes."

"This reading will help you understand that we don't die and that after-death communication is real. A true visitation from those in spirit will feel as if the person is really there with you."

"I didn't have that," Diana remarks, irritation evident in her voice.

"You will," I assure her. "When you go through a deeper psychological healing, you will feel him. I hesitate to use the word 'depression' with you but you have a low energy, emotionally, that has not yet cleared. When that lifts, you will be able to sense him."

I tune back in to hear more from Diana's husband. "He mentions a move, which relates to either him or you."

"That was one of my questions. I want to know if I should sell my home. I don't know what to do. I'm completely lost without him," Diana says, her voice trailing off.

"Well, he wants to come through with that because you've had that on your mind. He's aware of your thoughts and feelings. I sense that you aren't at the point to make a clear decision. What he shows me are scales, which are symbolic of weighing things or situations. One day your thoughts go this way and the next, the other way."

"He was a Libra, too!" Diana exclaims.

I was hopeful the dark clouds around her were starting to dissipate. "Oh, yes, Libra *is* the sign of the scales. Your move will have to evolve and things must line up for you to do that. Emotionally you are not in that space."

I am suddenly infused with a sense of peace that I feel Ed wants me to pass along to his wife. I try to put this feeling into words. "Let me explain this to you. When a person who is in a state of unease comes for a reading, the other side will come through with feelings about that. He is saying, 'Be at peace. Let it go.' It's the Big Picture they bring to us because sometimes we get stuck in our emotions. The feeling he is giving me is peace and he wants me to give that to you. You can recreate that feeling through acceptance of the ways things are now."

"Uh-huh," Diana utters softly.

Is she getting this? I wonder. "What do you do spiritually for yourself?"

"I pray, meditate and do yoga."

"Good, good."

"On the evening he died, he wanted me to sleep next to him. I hadn't been doing that for months since he was restless at night. He never wanted any pain medication. He told the doctor he wanted to die consciously. That last night, I sat up and watched him die right before my eyes. I wonder...did he die consciously?"

"Let me ask him." A minute or so goes by as I focus on what Ed is communicating about the end of his life. "He's making me feel as if he knew what was happening to him. Do you understand that your husband had fear about dying?"

"Totally, but it was not about being dead. It was the fear of suffocating."

"Yes. This fear was why he wanted to stay conscious for as long as possible. That's the best way I know to communicate that to you. He feared the pathway to death, not death itself."

"A few years ago, he had a near-death experience and said he came back to life because of me. This time he *didn't* come back."

That certainly explained a lot. Diana had expectations that Ed would again return and when he didn't she was understandably devastated. "My sense is that he came back the first time so the two of you would have more time together. That made it easier for you. He says he had other karma to finish here, as well."

A number suddenly appears in my mind. "Hmm . . . why would he be telling me about the number 10? And there is also a connection to October."

"He died on October 10, 2010."

"Wow! That's a strong validation."

"Yeah, it sure is. Will I be able to talk to him?"

"Oh, yes. A good way to do that is with a photograph and a candle. Go into meditation and ask him to be with you. The main ways you will connect with him are through feeling and intuition. The communication won't hit you over the head, such as seeing full-body materialization, for example. If you do this in the way I suggest, though, you will begin to open the relationship on a spiritual level. He adds that you wrote about him."

"I wrote a letter to him after he died. Was he there at his funeral when I put it in his casket?"

"Yes. That's why he brought that through. That is another way you can connect with him."

"Through writing?"

"Yes. It is also a way of healing your unresolved feelings."

The reading suddenly shifts when Diana asks if I feel there had been a past-life association between her and her husband. She explains that several years earlier, she had undergone a past-life regression, which revealed that she had once taken care of him until his death from a long-term illness. "When he died, I felt completely, utterly alone. That is how I feel now," she says through tears.

"Karmic relationships can repeat themselves, depending on whether we have learned the lesson involved. It could be that this time you still need to absorb the lesson of learning to let go. That was a soul agreement."

Diana's voice is strained as she continues. "I felt like I couldn't do anything about his death. I begged him not to die in front of me because I didn't want to go through that again, but he did it anyway!"

Clearly, she was taking her husband's death very personally. "Rarely do we understand karma as it plays out. You're right in the midst of grief. I recommend that you go into acceptance of his death. In that way, the karma can be healed. Here's another facet that he is making me feel answers a question: He says he'll be with you again. You might wonder what both of the lifetimes were presenting to you on a soul level. You are learning compassionate detachment; it is compassionate because of the soul mate connection between the two of you. Detachment happens when you understand the innate cycle of life and the soul's need to move on. It (the soul) returns when the time is right."

Diana is silent for a few moments as she absorbs this. I sense the light from the other side beginning to penetrate through the heavy wall of grief around her. The session is nearly over. I trust that even though it didn't seem apparent to me, Diana had received exactly what she needed from our time together.

"He's saying that he will impress you through inspiration with what way to go with your studies. Have you looked into anything at this point?"

"Many things. I want to go to naturopathic school but I can't afford it. I don't know what to do. Without him being here, I have no motivation."

"Well, motivation comes from within you. He simply reflected that motivation for you when he was here and he's still doing that. It's just in a different way. That's why the message was given, so you can recognize this inspiration when it happens."

"Does it bother him knowing that I can't feel him? Why can some people have visitations and other don't? He told me before he died that he would come back and visit me." I sense desperation in her voice.

"You're only six months into grieving. Give it time! If we hang expectations on things, we push them away. Believe me, he knows about your intent to hear from him."

The session ends with my giving Diana information about spirit guides and angels who are helping to heal her heart. In striking contrast to the subdued, sad demeanor she'd projected just an hour earlier, Diana thanks me warmly before hanging up. The contrast was so striking it was if I were talking to another person. Afterwards, I pondered what the reading revealed from a higher perspective than what had been obviously communicated. The spiritual seedlings that would eventually blossom into strength, acceptance and peace had been planted and nurtured over several lifetimes for both souls. I sensed it may be too soon for Diana to come to terms with it, but the love she shared with her late husband would remain with her forever, despite their temporary physical separation.

A Hug from Heaven

Over the years, I've been asked many times if the sensation of pain registers with people who die in physically traumatic ways such as car accidents, murders or suicides. In all the readings I've done, I have seen quite the contrary. Souls who have died in this way have described leaving their bodies a few seconds before the awareness of crushing pain registers with their conscious minds. The following transcript is taken from a reading with a woman who had uncertainty about her granddaughter's death—specifically, whether she had suffered extensive physical pain in the accident that claimed her life.

"I don't want to tell you anything except that I had a devastating loss last year," says Trudy, a well-dressed, polite woman in her late sixties.

"Okay," I respond. "I just want to know if you have life issues you want me to focus on or if you want spirit communication only."

"The latter," Trudy says pointedly.

"There is a contemporary male energy in your generation coming through for you."

"Uh, I lost a brother a long time ago. I also had a dear friend my age who passed."

"Hold on," I say as I tune in to establish the spirit's identity. "He says he was connected to business. Did he own his own business?"

Trudy's business-like demeanor suddenly changes and she starts to cry. "I think this is my very dear friend."

"He dresses like a businessman with a long coat and dress hat. I feel it's his way of communicating that he was a professional man. He says you worked with him in the business. He comes today in support of you."

"Yes, I did work with him."

"I'm also hearing the names of Bill and Louise."

"Bill is my uncle. I didn't really know him. Louise is my mother who passed."

"I see. They are coming here as support to let you know they are there for you spiritually. Your mother steps forward as a primary communicator here and says that your loss is the worst thing that could happen. In fact, you've thought and said that very thing."

"Yes, I have."

"Your mom talks about the younger energy that is with her. This person is younger than her and you. To you, that is a child, grandchild, niece or nephew. She says that is the reason you're here."

Trudy's eyes fill with tears. "Yes," she whispers.

"Let me see if the younger energy will talk with me. There was an extremely rapid passing here. Not sure if this is a male or female."

"Yes, my granddaughter," Trudy adds, fighting back tears. She seems to want to hold her composure.

"She is with your mom. She is making me feel there was a tragic, emotional charge to this passing. Guilt, anger, blame . . . I'm not sure but this is what she communicates. These are somehow attached to her passing."

"Blame. I blamed myself for not calling her before she died."

"Uh-huh. You've beat yourself up thinking that you should have been there for her."

"Right. I should have been there to make sure she was safe."

"You never got to say goodbye. There's a lack of closure and guilt on top of that. That's the emotional charge she refers to."

"Yes, it's true."

"Someone talks of passing near a holiday or significant date."

"That's my brother. He passed on Holy Thursday, right before

Easter."

"That's his way of saying he is with your granddaughter, as well. She comes through as very vibrant, smart and having every reason to live. People have asked why this would happen to someone who had everything going for her. In fact, Spirit is impressing me that someone in the family had a crisis of faith because of her passing."

"Her mom did."

"She gives that message because she wants to let you know she's aware of her mom's feelings. This does, by the way, come through to me as an accidental passing."

Suddenly, the young woman in spirit persists in causing me to feel that the nature of the accident was odd. I pass this information along to Trudy. "It has a 'freakish' feel to it; you can't understand how it occurred. You've thought, *How could this even happen? It's so bizarre.*"

"Yes, it was a bizarre accident."

"She shows me a large question mark around her death, as well. There are a lot of questions about her death."

Trudy sighs and nods. "The people who went to her aid said they did not understand how the accident happened."

"Yes, it was freakish she says."

Trudy offers no explanation but says, "Can I ask her a question?"

"Hold on for one second. I don't want to lose my link with her. She says she was gone, even though there were attempts to revive her. She says she stayed there with her body but was detached from it."

Trudy is persistent in her attempt to find out what happened to cause the accident. "Did she fall asleep?"

I mentally ask the young woman this question. "The feeling she gives me is that there will always be unanswered questions about that. You've lied awake at night wondering what happened. There's a message about crossing a center line on the road. Did someone do that?"

"She did."

"I am not hearing about her falling asleep. She says she veered over the center line but doesn't say why. She talks about the family and her life in college. She was on the honor roll, an achiever."

"Yes!"

"She wants you to know she didn't suffer when she passed."

With the delivery of this message, Trudy cries. "That answers one of the questions I wrote down before our reading. I wanted to know that."

"She answered that before you had a chance to ask about it today," I tell her.

An image of a gold necklace enters my mind. I describe this to Trudy.

"I had planned on giving her this," she says, reaching for the same gold necklace around her neck. "It was my dad's. I never take it off. I touch it a lot and think about my dad."

"That's what she's referring to. I also feel it's your dad's way of coming through here, as well." I paused as the young woman impresses me with another message. "Your granddaughter is making a reference to writing. And there is some sort of teaching connection, as well."

Trudy laughs. "I don't know if this is what she is referring to but after she died, her mother shared with us that she kept a daily planner where she wrote about everything in her life. We all found it humorous that she wrote about incidental things such as what TV shows she watched and what time she shaved her legs. It was hysterical to all of us that she wrote about the precise time she wanted to shave her legs."

"So this was somewhat of a family joke, wasn't it?"

"Yes, but in a loving way."

"That is why she is making reference to it. You all knew about this after her passing."

Trudy's face lights up. "Oh, she *did* help her mother to write papers. She's still going to school."

"She says her mother is a teacher."

"Her mother is studying for her doctorate degree and is a teacher."

"This is all validation to let you know she's around the family," I explain.

"I have a question: Did she come to me in November?"

"I don't want to just say 'yes.' I want her to give me something to validate that for you." After a few seconds, I add: "There are a couple of things she is mentioning. One of them is that she comes to you at night, in dreams or by impressing you with her presence when you are waking up. She also shows me that she is with the family on holidays."

"Just last Thanksgiving we lit a candle on the table in her memory."

"She says that was her presence there with the family. She wanted to let you know that she knows about that. The last thing I want to leave you with is a name: Karen."

Trudy thought for a moment. "Oh, I have a close friend by that name who just had surgery."

"It's a validation to let you know your granddaughter is aware of recent events in your life."

The final message of the session is a poignant one for Trudy: It comes to me through an odd sensation of two arms wrapped around my shoulders.

"In closing, I feel that she is hugging me and wants me to pass that along to you."

Tears immediately spill from Trudy's eyes. For several minutes she is unable to speak. Finally, she says, "I've felt her do that to me before! I heard her call my name and put her arms around me. I don't think anyone believes me, but it's true."

"I believe you," I assure her. "I've read for others who described these hugs from heaven. I'm leaving all of this with you with Spirit's great love and blessings."

The Surfer

I sometimes read for people who harbor anger concerning the loss of a loved one. Although it is normal to have such feelings in the grieving process, carrying them for extended periods of time eventually becomes detrimental to one's well being. As long as we stubbornly cling to anger, we remain in resistance to the higher truth of a situation. If we understand that we have no control over others or situations outside of ourselves, we can move beyond anger into acceptance and healing. The following communication from a session with Maggie and her cousin, Lora, contains insightful teachings from the spirit world about letting go of anger and taking personal responsibility from Maggie's son in spirit.

As the reading begins, I am bombarded with evidential information from various spirits, and I rely on Maggie and Lora to help me determine whom each message is for. Many souls—grandparents, great-aunts and uncles—come through for the two women during the next 15 minutes. Each comes through with a name and illness that they had died from. Still, I sense there is someone who has not yet shown up, someone who both women want to hear from. I am grateful that this is my last reading for the day, as I feel it's going to be a doozy. I take a deep breath and continue to relate what I perceive.

"I'm hearing from your mother, Maggie, about this coming August being significant with people getting together. These are family members you've not seen for awhile or you may receive some sort of communication from."

Maggie's eyes widen in anticipation. "We're thinking about doing something in August."

"A family reunion?"

"No, it's more of a memorial. Do you pick up on any feelings around that?"

"I am given a feeling that there could be more than one person memorialized at this service or that there is a dual purpose to the event."

"That makes sense," Lora says excitedly.

"There is a feeling that the service you have planned brings finalization, putting things to rest and peace regarding certain family members. You're at the end of a cycle. That applies to you, especially, Maggie."

Maggie is silent but nods in agreement.

"Further, I'm being shown that you will get property or something else that comes back to you related to the memorial. It's as if you are saying *Now I have this back and I can rest.* The cycle is then complete, your mother says."

"That all makes sense. Does my mom have anyone there with her?"

I take another deep breath and tune in. "She gives me the feeling that a younger energy is being acknowledged."

"Yes."

"To you, this is a child, niece or nephew."

"My son."

"It makes sense now why so many older family members are coming through. They want to show you that they are with you as pillars of strength after your traumatic loss. I sense that both of you come from families who were survivors of hard times. Your son is with your mom, Maggie. She says that she lets you know she's with you by causing a tingling sensation around your hair and shoulders."

"That happened to me here tonight!"

"It's her way of bringing you comfort." At that moment, I become aware of yet another spirit stepping into the reading. "There's a young woman who stands beside your son in spirit. He is bringing her through. Has someone else in the family lost a child?"

My question hangs in the air as Maggie and Lora look at one

another in bewilderment. "No, not that we know of," Lora finally responds.

"Well, she is here and says she is somehow connected to your son. Do you know the parent of this girl?"

Maggie ponders for a moment. "Yes! I think I do. I didn't know the girl, but my son did."

I ask for more information to validate the relationship of these two spirits. "Someone passed very quickly." Next, I feel the familiar fuzziness in my head that signals drugs or alcohol was directly involved in the passing. "Which one used substances?"

"Both of them," Maggie replies, her voice beginning to crack with emotion.

"Now I understand how they knew one another. Tell the girl's mom she is with your son. When I connect with him, my emotions feel as if they are in turmoil. He says that's the way he was before he died. There was a period of darkness preceding his death. He shows me that there had been a falling out between him and you or with his dad. Then he died."

"Yes, they had an argument just prior to his death," Maggie confirms.

"Then he passed. That's the period of darkness he is referring to."

"He and I also had a disagreement before he passed," Maggie adds.

"You go over that a lot in your mind."

"Yes."

"He says you're going to counseling for this."

"I'm starting a support group with mothers of children who passed in the same way. The mother of the girl you saw my son with is in this group."

"I see. Please tell her that her daughter came through here. Your son makes me feel as if he had other mental and emotional problems besides substance abuse. It feels like depression."

"He had anxiety and depression."

"He points to those as factors in his drug use. He doesn't give me the feeling that this was intentional."

"Yes, it was ruled accidental."

"He is pointing at himself as being responsible for his death."

Maggie frowns. "So he doesn't want us to try and pursue anyone else?" she asks.

"No. The feeling he gives me is that the drugs he took interacted with other drugs in his system."

"That's absolutely right. But someone gave him another substance that he had never taken before. They misled him!" Maggie replied angrily, her eyes flaring.

"I get that," I convey, "but it wouldn't do any good to pursue anyone else. He says it would be a dead-end."

This message evokes even a stronger emotional response in Maggie. "What about the people who were present who ignored his distress and didn't call 911?" she asks.

The next message is startlingly clear: "Yes, but he's making me feel as if going after them legally would create much more stress and pain for the family to go through than it would be worth. This is not about money for you. It's about justice for your son. But the others involved will have to pay for what they did through cosmic justice, or karma. You have had to cycle through many emotions to come to terms with this. There's much anger with you, anger at these people and at your son for what he did," I say, looking directly at her.

Maggie returns my stare, while Lora looks down at the floor. For a moment, I feel as if she is challenging me. Neither say anything in acknowledgment yet I know that last message hit them hard.

Finally Maggie speaks up. "Is he happy?"

The compelling message from Maggie's son about personal responsibility continues in spite of her question. At this moment, I feel the need to share personal experience from my work in order to help her understand. "Over the years, I've never communicated with a spirit who was happy about ending his life prematurely. Your son sees the implications of the choices he made. He wanted to please the people he was with at the time of his death (so he took the drugs.) He didn't want to appear weak. Still, he made the choice to do what he did."

Maggie and Lora sit quietly and listen intently. "The memorial that your mom referenced earlier—it's for your son, isn't it?"

"Yes, it's for his friends."

"Your son shows me a connection with the beach."

Maggie gasps. "That's it! He was a surfer. We're going out on a boat and we're taking his surfboard with us in his memory."

"That's a very nice tribute. He wants you to remember him like that. That's when he was peaceful and happy."

"He is saying that he felt most peaceful when he was surfing."

"Is he peaceful now? Does he still feel the same struggles as when he was here?"

"No. When we pass, we have the life review where we are shown how our choices affected others. Your son has seen all of this. He's come to an acceptance of the spiritual life lessons he was presented with. No condition that we experience—mental, emotional or physical—is by chance."

"So you mean before we're born we select those issues we need to work on?" Maggie interjects.

"Yes. There are certain things that we agree to experience here. Your son was highly creative, fun loving, well liked and sensitive. He had all of that going for him. But there was a side to his sensitivity that he did not know how to deal with. Because of that, he was affected by the outside world. It became somewhat overwhelming to him. He had problems dealing with this and wanted to have a different mindset. So he made the choice to use drugs. On the other side, he's had to take a look at that."

"Does he come to us in ways we would recognize?"

A few seconds after Maggie asks this, an image of sand comes into my mind. "He gives me the feeling that someone drew or created something in the sand." I zero in for more information. "Hmm... I don't know if someone is going to do this, but he mentions someone building something in the sand. This is related to him."

Maggie's eyes grow large. "I know exactly what that is! His brother was in Hawaii. He took his shirt off and laid it in the sand. Then he placed a pair of swimming trunks with his sunglasses on top. It looked as if he had just jumped out of his clothes. His brother thought this was funny and took a picture of it. The figure in the sand was to represent his brother [in spirit.]"

"He's making me feel that his dad needs to go to counseling since he finds it hard to talk about his feelings."

"I know he does. Do my loved ones who came through express that they love me or is that just a given?" Maggie asks.

"We haven't closed the session yet. Let me explain. During a session, I'm infused with emotion that I have to put into language to give to you. Usually it comes at the end when they show me symbols, such as roses, that they hand to you. Your son is handing you photographs."

Upon hearing this, both women giggle. I sense they think it's an odd message. I feel the heavy energy of the session begin to lift as I explain to them what the photos symbolize.

"Besides your eternal relationship with him, you have physical things like photos that connect you with him. You look at those all the time, he says. You think of him and talk to him. He feels that. There's love being expressed with that. Your other relatives that came through tonight expressed love by their very presence. This is all about love. Both of your families were strong. They were survivors. You've had to draw on the strength of your ancestors to get through the tragedy of losing a child. Know that they're there for you."

It is the end of the evening and I am tired. Before leaving, Maggie tells me that she has a new perspective about her son's tragic death and that she would reconsider bringing suit against the people who had given him drugs. I urge both women to listen to the audio file of the session so that none of the validations and wisdom coming from their loved ones would be missed. I bid them good-bye, lock my office door for the evening and head home. For me, it was simply the end of another day of doing my life's work. But for the two women who had just heard from their loved ones, it could very well be the dawn of a new day.

Dad, Did You Love Me?

Every so often, people ask for insights about dreams they've had in which relationships with deceased loved ones take center stage. The following session illustrates how a woman's dream played a key role in understanding and healing her emotions towards her late father.

"Where are you calling in from today?" I ask Val, my noon phone appointment.

"Georgia," she responds. "It's a beautiful day here and I'm sitting outside talking to you. The reason I'm calling you is to understand something. I had a dream in which my late father was hollering at my mother. He turned around and started yelling at me. My skin was tingling because I was so afraid. In my mind, I told myself, *This is a dream! Wake up!* I didn't want to listen to him anymore. I thought, *What were you trying to tell me, Dad? Why were you so mad at Mom?* So I'm wondering what he wanted to tell me."

As Val tells her story, an image of a man with an angry scowl on his face pops into my mind. One thing's for sure: this man had not been happy during life.

I relay what I feel to Val.

"Uh, yeah. I never knew him to be happy."

"He's been coming around you, mainly through feelings. When we sleep, we are open to visitations from the other side, but we also process our emotions. Your dad is saying that he's now aware of his behavior while on earth. He's had to come to terms with how he acted when he was here. There was a lot of bitterness, resentment and a self-serving attitude. He shows me that he was very controlling. He really wants to communicate that he's completely embarrassed and ashamed of his behavior. You've already done healing around that, he says, through therapy or just working it out in your mind. Did you feel at some point that you wished you would have done more for your mom?"

"No. She was a very strong woman," Val replies. "I think my dad thought I was like her. If he got upset with her, he would get upset with me. I didn't do anything to justify that. I felt like a mini-version of my mom."

"The point of this is that since his death, you've been coming to terms with the fact that the problem was within your dad, not you or your mom. You've had a long time to realize that there was nothing flawed—and there never has been—about you. That's the reckoning, the awakening, within you. Your dad echoes that. The dream is just one of many times he's come to you inspirationally. He wants you to understand how messed up emotionally he was from his family."

"Yes, I knew that. I want to ask him a question because I need to finalize things in my life," Val says, her voice thick with emotion. At the same time, I detect a vague apprehension coming from her.

"Go ahead," I tell her.

"Dad, did you really love me?"

It's a simple, pure question, yet one loaded with years of desperation and uncertainty. At that moment, I feel her pain. I know this question requires more than a simple "yes" response in order for her to understand. I wait a few seconds before responding and focus on what I'm feeling.

"The message I conveyed to you about his being able to see his own behavior now is part of the answer. This reading is a verbal confirmation of what you've already been given through your intuition. The message is that he's taking responsibility for his own actions. He also points to his family, his ancestors, who were emotionally unbalanced. I hope you can verify that. Are you aware of that?"

Val is silent for a moment. "Well, I think it's depression and anxiety. I have those, too."

"Yes, he's showing the ancestry as an explanation of conditions that were factors in his treatment of you. You have taken steps to improve that. Haven't you gone through therapy?"

"Oh, yes!"

"That's what he's saying. Your healing began a long time ago. All you have done in that way has affected and helped your ancestors who didn't do that when they were here, including him. They never stepped up to the plate and said, 'I want a better life.' You have said, 'I don't want to live like that.' He makes me feel that you have written a final chapter in your paternal line as far as the heavy, dysfunctional energy that was present. The dream you had was another level of that."

"Okay."

"It's not so much the practical end of things that he didn't take responsibility for when he was here. It's the *emotional* end of things that he didn't do. Do you get that?"

"Yes."

"He says he screwed up and he points to his parents who affected him. He's had to process that on the other side. Generationally, you absorbed much of the emotional impact of the family. This is the end of the cycle. Do you have a son?"

"Yes."

"Your dad mentions him and says he won't carry this energy. He's a different temperament."

"Yes, I understand that."

"Is there a grandson for you yet? If there isn't he says there will be."

"Well, I wanted to ask that, too. My youngest son and his wife have tried so hard to have a baby and it hasn't happened. Will they?"

"Your dad is pointing that out by saying there will be a grandson for you. He makes me feel that he is giving that message in response to this question you wanted to ask in our session today."

"But they've tried everything to conceive and it hasn't happened," Val adds with agitation.

"Adoption may be the answer. Keep open to that possibility. It's really ironic that when we try too hard, we block something from happening. He mentions Philip. Who is that?"

"Uh, he's the grandfather of the children I watch. I'm a nanny. I just saw him last week. He told me the kids were lucky to have someone who took good care of them."

"Your dad is holding that up as positive quality about you. You and I just spoke about how he didn't treat you so well when he was here. In contrast, he's referencing this conversation with Philip as a validation of how good you are. He is aware of what your life is like now. Believe it or not, he sees your goodness, your light. You didn't hear that when he was here."

"That's great to hear now."

"As further validation, he says that you'll get a bonus or pay raise from taking care of the kids."

"I just got a raise!"

"He says to look at the good job you're doing. You never got that when he was here. Your dad has done much healing in spirit. You need to know that."

From the other end of the phone, I feel the incredible impact these words are having on Val. "Wow!" is all she can utter.

"On a spiritual level, your lessons with your dad have helped you to build self-love. If you didn't have a father like him, you wouldn't have had to rely on yourself. Do you understand?"

"Yes."

"People beat themselves up for years wondering why they

have a tough relationship with a parent. They ask, 'Why do I feel as if he never really loved me?' If we look at this on a soul level, we can understand why. You've done a remarkable job in giving and expressing love to others. I just heard the name Don."

"That's amazing! That's the little boy I care for in my job. He and I have a very special bond."

"See? Your dad knows about all of this. He holds this boy up as another example of your ability to love."

Near the end of the session, Val's dad leaves her with a compelling message: "He says that you've developed a strong ability to love, especially children, because you know what it's like to not receive that from a parent. He shows me that you've vowed to make sure your own children know that you're there for them. Your dad is aware of your love and compassion."

Before we hang up, I suggest to Val that she write these words on a piece of paper: *Dad, I forgive you. I love you. Thank you for doing the best that you possibly could. Love, Val.* I advise her to then take the paper outside and burn it to symbolize her release from all negative feelings towards her dad. Although many miles separate us during the reading, I feel the immense relief in Val's voice as she thanks me. Hearing from her dad seems to have dissolved years of uncertainty and anguish. Somewhere in Georgia a healing was taking place.

Eight

Life Lessons

Love is a portion of the soul itself, and it is of the same nature as the celestial breathing of the atmosphere of paradise.
Victor Hugo

A few years ago, I created a workshop called *Understanding Death from a Spiritual Perspective* to help people cope with grief. One of the exercises in the workshop involves writing a letter of gratitude to the deceased loved one. As guidelines, I present students with several questions:

1. *If the person in spirit were sitting across from me now, what would I want to communicate?*
2. *How would this person want me to remember him or her?*
3. *What did I learn from our relationship?*
4. *How did my loved one's life touch or heal others?*

During the exercise, I play soft music and encourage people to look into the eyes of their deceased loved one in the photograph I've asked them to bring. Afterwards, we discuss the feelings and insights that came up for everyone. Most participants have reported that this exercise gives them a much deeper under-standing of the *spiritual* meaning of their loved one's life and their relationship. Participants have also commented about gaining greater peace while moving through grief.

Long ago, my spirit guides used the simple analogy of ripples emanating from a stone thrown into water to illustrate how our lives affect others. They also impressed on me that when we return to our home in the spirit world, we see precisely how our lives have touched others. They also told me that our parents see the lives of their children when they die. Over the course of many readings, I have seen how true this is. Our lives are not separate from others; we are all part of the great, all-encompassing unity of life. The intuitive recognition of this fact is all we ever really need to realize in order to give love and service without compromise.

The stories in this chapter illustrate how souls from the other side come through with a spiritually centered, panoramic vision of their lives on the physical plane. Each reading is unique yet all contain the theme of life lessons from a spiritual perspective. The first reading exemplifies how a woman's care of her mother helped to positively change her career.

Mom, You've Inspired Me to Help Others

The next reading made an impression on me because it highlights three significant spiritual qualities: forgiveness, compassion and transformation. It is a shining example of how trying situations in life, such as family disputes and taking care of a dying loved one, can be turned into positive ones if we open ourselves to see beyond the challenges. During this session, I was struck with the amount of fortitude, love and peace that emanated from my client, Sharon. I chose to include her story here so that others who are or have been caretakers of loved ones with debilitating conditions and illnesses may find hope, comfort and strength, despite the apparent challenges.

"I'm aware of the cancer passing. Who would that have been?" I ask Sharon, a neatly dressed, strikingly attractive woman with a pleasant smile.

"My mother," she says immediately.

"Okay. You know, I was aware of her on your right side when I was saying my prayer." Immediately, I begin to receive impressions from another female. "There's a contemporary woman who is with your mom; a sister, sister-in-law or close friend."

"She has no sisters, so it must be Mom's best friend," Sharon answers. "They were friends for years."

"She says she is happy to be reunited with her. She also acknowledges a woman whose name begins with the letters A-L."

Sharon thinks for a moment before responding, "My aunt Alice. She is still here."

"How's her health? That's usually the reason someone living is named in a reading."

"Well, she has late stage multiple sclerosis."

"Your mom is saying that the family will be there when it's her time to pass. They will help her with the transition."

A clairvoyant image floats into my awareness. "I am seeing the letters V-A. Was someone a veteran?"

"My father was."

"That would be his way of coming through today. Your mom was bringing him through. Also someone is here with the initial J."

"That's my sister-in-law, Jan! She was my very best friend."

"When she passed, you felt as if a part of you had left. She says she connects with you through scent. This will be an 'internal' smell of flowers or perfume. There's an emphasis about perfume, by the way. Do you understand this?"

Sharon starts to laugh in recognition. "We were shopping one day and I told her she needed to splurge on herself. I told her about a perfume that I thought she would like. When she smelled it, she loved it and bought it. Now, every time I open a magazine with the perfume samples inside, I think of her."

"That's what she means. That's one of the ways she'll connect with you. She also shows me a silk scarf."

"She gifted me with a silk scarf that her cousin made. I've wear it a lot."

"She infuses me with love for you." The communication flows on. "William or Bill is mentioned."

"That's my husband," Sharon responds.

Sharon's mother is a strong communicator. The validations she gives are quick and easily recognizable. She obviously wants her daughter to know that she is speaking with her. "She's with the man who passed from lung and heart problems."

"My father-in-law."

"You mom says she's been with you since she passed and has communicated to someone in the family through a dream. You will also perceive her through emotions. She comes through to you with a strong, feeling nature. Love, compassion . . . that's how she will communicate with you. She says there's a significant date around this time as far as a birthday or a death goes."

"Both her and my step-father, who is still alive, had the same birthday, which is next week."

"She makes me feel that you need to look in on him. Some healing needs to be sent in his direction. His health may not be good. Do you still have contact with him?"

Sharon's pleasant demeanor suddenly changes. "I do," she says in a subdued voice.

"The relationship has been difficult, hasn't it?"

"Yes, there have been difficulties."

"That's where the healing comes in; it's more of an emotional thing. She's making me feel as if you need to take things with a grain of salt as far as his personality is concerned. She doesn't say exactly what the issue is, but do you feel as if he took advantage of her when they were married?"

"He took advantage of her being gone. He disrespected her wishes in the will."

"She's saying that there is something that will occur that will heal this situation. You may hear from him about all of this. She says there will be an opportunity to make peace here. She makes me feel he has withdrawn from the family after her death. He moved, didn't he?"

"Yes," Sharon says under her breath.

"In these types of situations, you have to accept what is. She's not saying what he did was okay; rather she's now coming from a point of greater understanding. She says that there were some decisions made about her well being that the family didn't agree upon."

"My step-father had very little to say about her care. We had to teach him what to do."

"Did you notice he started to pull back at that point?"

"No, he would have done anything to help her. What was frustrating was that he never understood what we explained to him. He didn't understand a lot."

"Thanks for clarifying this. She gives me the feeling that this whole falling out started awhile ago. In other words, it didn't begin after she passed. She clearly is making me feel that something wasn't right about her care. There's a lack of peace with it."

"My mom and step-father stayed with my brother, who had just lost his wife, Jan. During that period when we were mourning her, my brother was behaving in ways that were difficult for us to accept. This bothered my mom. She was restless in her final hours. I made my brother go in and make things right with her. As soon as he did that, she passed peacefully."

"This whole reference of unrest is being brought up in order for you to heal it. You can then move beyond it. She's forgiven it. You wanted to make sure your mom had the optimal care for her illness. She is emphasizing that you made that happen. Regardless of what else went on, you made sure that happened. Again she says there will be an opportunity to clarify and forgive with these people."

"My step-father sold all of the contents of her home, and cashed in all their savings and investments. He cannot understand now why no one in the family wants to communicate with him. I'm the only one who will."

"She says that you need to remain open when the healing opportunity comes. She says that some of what was lost, such as her belongings, will come back."

"I'm hearing the name Katherine. Who is that?"

"That's my middle name. My mom called me by that all the time!" Sharon says excitedly.

"She tells me that's a way you would know it's her," I explain.

Before the reading ends, Sharon's mother gives several messages about other family members which Sharon validates. Then she reiterates her prior message: "There will be a shift in your family in September as far as a healing opportunity is concerned."

Afterwards, Sharon, a registered nurse who formerly worked in occupational therapy, tells me how taking care of her mother was a life-changing experience that led her to change her career focus to end-of-life care. During her mom's illness, she says that she focused not only on her physical care, but also on her emotional and spiritual well being. As we speak, I notice Sharon's eyes light up with appreciation for the growth she gained through a trying circumstance. No resentment or bitterness was evident; there was only gratitude for the experience. In fact, as a result of taking care of her mom, Sharon became aware of a need for better hospice care for others and soon sought training to learn those services. Currently, she's using her skills and experience as an advocate and educator for hospice services to healthcare organizations.

The Man in Scrubs

As mentioned earlier, we are shown how our life has touched the lives of others after we cross over, similar to George Bailey in *It's a Wonderful Life*. The next reading features communication with a soul who had made significant contributions to others through his work as a doctor. From the other side, he promises to help his widow in her own healing practice.

"Can I tell you who I want to connect with?" asks Tonya before I begin her phone reading. Her voice—upbeat and perky with a discernible Italian accent—contains none of the heaviness I typically feel from people in grief. For a moment, I consider her question.

"No, not unless they don't come through," I answer. "Let's see what happens first."

I say my prayer and jump in. "An older male is here. He comes through feeling like a father to you."

"That's my grandfather on my mom's side. He was like a father to me."

Other validations follow, all from members of Tonya's sizable family in spirit. Then I receive this message: "Someone is involved in healthcare. Who is that?"

"My husband. Well, really we both are," Tonya answers. "But I haven't worked in the field for awhile. I do energy healing, reiki and theta healing."

"There's a message that his place of work has or will change. I'm hearing that the number five is significant to someone's passing. It's directly connected to you or your husband. Can you identify that?"

"I don't know. Can I tell you something?" Tonya asks insistently.

I sense that she is going to reveal details about herself or her husband that I would rather get from Spirit to maintain the integrity of the reading. "No," I say firmly yet gently. "Let's continue."

After giving identity of Tonya's mother-in-law in spirit, I say, "Tell your husband his mother came through."

"I have to tell you this, Carole, I have to. Can I just tell you?" Tonya pleads.

Before I can answer, she blurts out, "My husband died four weeks ago in an accident."

"Oh, my gosh!" I am surprised by this disclosure and at the

same time not, since many spirits who've recently passed (less than a month) do not typically connect with me during readings. (I believe this is due to their need to adjust to the spirit world and "decompress" from physical life. Because of this, I suggest that people wait at least several months after a loss before having a reading. This also gives clients time to work through the initial stages of grieving which can help in the communication process during readings.)

"I'm going to start crying because . . . "

"Hold on!" I interrupt. "Don't tell me anything more! This explains why your mother-in-law is coming through. He's with her."

I focus on what I see with my inner vision. "He's making me feel as if his passing was rough. There's a sensation of being thrown. Can you validate that?"

"Yes, he was thrown off of his motorcycle. It was a collision with another vehicle."

"He says that before he even hit the ground, he was gone from his body."

"You mean his soul was out of his body?"

"Yes. I've seen this in similar passings. The soul is catapulted out of the body before any pain registers. He says someone tried to bring him back but he was gone."

"Yeah, there was an attempt."

"He says you recently contacted an attorney. I'm sorry to get into this topic at this stage of the game since it's really early in the grieving process for you."

"That's okay. Yes, I did contact an attorney. I talked to someone about a wrongful death suit. He was at the peak of his life, only 48. It won't bring him back, I know. The money [from the suit] would be for our children for college. People ask me why I don't cry more since he died. I say, 'Why? It won't bring him back.'"

I am stunned- not from the disclosure that Tonya's husband

had passed, but by how remarkably well she seemed to be doing following such a recent, devastating loss. Still, I know that she contacted me for evidence that her husband lives on in spirit. I reach inside for something to give her.

"He says that you used to worry a lot about him riding a motorcycle."

"Always! Of course, I did. The last words I said to him on the day he died were, 'Please be very, very careful on the motor-cycle'."

"He impresses me that he will communicate with you through music and numbers—on license plates and clocks. The numbers will repeat and they will be synchronistic. He says that he visited you recently in a dream."

"Yes, he's come to me. Here's what happened," Tonya explains, speaking rapidly. "This past week was the fifth week since he's been gone and . . . "

"That's the number five reference I just mentioned a few moments ago," I remind her.

"Oh! Yes, of course. Anyway, since he died, my heart has felt like it's in murky, dirty water. In the dream, I saw him lift up my heart from the water. It was not in the shape of a valentine; it was a beating, anatomical heart. There was a bookcase with three shelves. The lowest one was in the murky water. I noticed the top shelf and I thought that one is not for me yet. He then placed my heart on the middle shelf. The next day, I felt very strong. I have not returned to the murky level- emotionally speaking- since."

I wait a few moments before responding. The dream clearly spoke for itself and explained why she carried little of the heaviness I've witnessed with other clients, especially after losing someone recently and unexpectedly. I sense that Tonya's dream was a pivotal point in the acceptance of her husband's death. "That's a profound dream. Let me maintain the connection with him so I don't lose it." A clairvoyant image appears in my mind. "Why would I be seeing him in scrubs?"

"He was a doctor," she answers matter-of-factly.

Suddenly it dawns on me that this spirit had been trying to identify himself earlier in the reading when I gave the messages about someone working in healthcare and the number five. Although she partially validated the first message, Tonya had not realized it was her husband's way of coming through in the reading, even though he was the primary person she wanted to hear from. He was trying to identify himself. Just as he had communicated earlier, the "location" of his work definitely had changed.

"He's saying that since he passed, he's seen the number of people he's helped here by being a doctor," I continue. "That came through his life review on the other side. He says that at one time, he worked with emergency medicine."

"Well, he was an orthopedic surgeon and he would set broken bones in the emergency room."

As the communication continues, the man imbues me with details about his life and personality. "He was incredibly bright and wants me to mention that he wrote something, a project that was close to his heart, even though he didn't get to finish it."

"Yes, he had started writing a book about different religions. It was something he loved."

"You helped him to understand other forms of healing. There was a lot that the two of you shared. He was a very spiritually based man. He credits Spirit for healing people through him in his medical practice. He says that he will continue to help you in your energy healing practice. He will be trained and working in that capacity on the other side."

"I believe it."

"You'll feel his presence in your hands and around your neck and shoulder area as you do your healing work. He mentions someone by the name of Nick. Do you know who this is?"

"I just took my youngest daughter to talk with Nick yesterday. He's a zoologist and she wants to do that, too."

"That's why he mentions it. It just happened. He adds that someone had or is going to have a medical discovery. It feels like an invention of some sort, a patent."

"That was my husband. He invented many things."

"Remember the message I gave you about his seeing the number of people he helped while on earth? That applies here-to his medical inventions. These are people he will never meet, yet his life and work here touched. This is all connected to the service he did when he was here."

On the other end of the phone, I hear Tonya sniffle, indicating that the last message was making an emotional impact her. "Oh, yes! He did so much in his young life."

I become aware of the magnitude of this man's spiritual consciousness, especially regarding his work as a doctor. "He was an advanced soul. The two of you go way back in time together. He shows me what is called the 'ripple effect', the analogy of throwing a stone in the water and watching it ripple out. That's what his work was like here."

Tonya seems to grasp all of this. She quickly proceeds to another area of concern in her life. "A little while ago, I was meditating and I heard my husband say he was sending someone else for me to love. I told him that I don't want that. I would always compare that person to him. He said, 'You're not the type of person to be alone. This person will be good for you and for the kids.' I was wondering if he could say anything more about that?"

"My impression is that it won't be too far off that you meet someone and get married again. Yes, he says he will be sending you someone."

"In some ways, I'm ashamed to feel open to that. But I know he would send someone to me. After all, he's not coming back."

"Spiritually speaking, he makes me feel that the two of you were learning harmony, compatibility and service work. You're both from a soul group whose work is to pave new ground and do healing. You learned compassion, nurturing and companionship with each other. Much of the karma each of you had was taken care of before meeting each other."

"Yes, we were like two peas in a pod."

As the session wraps, Tonya's husband leaves her with an inspiring message. "You will help many people with your hands-on healing work. I will be with you as you do that."

After the reading, Tonya tells me that she plans to continue doing the healing work that she loves. She feels it is one of the best ways to honor the memory of her husband. A week later and several times after that, she contacted me and offered to do distance healing for me, but our schedules didn't mesh. Then she emailed and told me her young son who was in remission from cancer had a flare-up and had to hospitalized. That is the last I heard from her. In retrospect, it's occurred to me that when Tonya's husband came through in the reading, perhaps he was guiding her to use her healing abilities on their son and impressing her that he would help from the other side. One thing was clear: despite his early death, this doctor's legacy of service to others would undoubtedly live on.

Go Have Fun!

I first met Susan through a local yoga studio where I did a group message program. Because I meet many people through my work and don't remember many of the readings, I did not recall our connection when she came for a private session a few months later. The following session is one of several with Susan that made a strong impression on me because of the extraordinary evidential details it contains. Although it doesn't contain information about unhealed emotional business, it beautifully illustrates the bond of undying love and friendship between mother and daughter.

"Your mom is here. I don't know how often you feel her, but . . ."

"Constantly," Susan blurts out.

I immediately sense that the woman in spirit is a vibrant communicator. In fact, she is so strong, it feels as if she is right beside me, whispering in my ear. A colorful clairvoyant image quickly materializes in my mind. "Why would she be showing me geraniums?"

Susan chuckles. "I'm trying to save her geranium plant. I got some information on the Internet about cutting it back to revive it. I just did that a couple of days ago."

"Since I did another reading for you six months ago, I asked your mom to bring through recent events in your life so you'll know she's around. I had to ask her to step it up a few notches as far as the communication goes. Your mom says she loved flowers. She'll come to you through scent."

"I have sinus problems so how can I . . . "

"This is not a physical scent; it's a memory, an internal sensation."

"Oh, okay."

"Now she shows me violets."

"That was her name- Violet!"

"Did that come through in our other reading?"

"No, it didn't. I also have one of her African violets. I've been cleaning out her house to sell it and I'm saving everything that has violets on it, including wall hangings and plaques."

"In two months she shows me that you are in a clear space with that property."

"Good! There is a young couple interested that I have a very positive feeling about."

The clarity of Violet's thoughts is astounding. "Your mom is with other women in her generation who have passed. Betsy is here. Ellen is also mentioned. Harry is with them."

"My aunt Betsy is her sister-in-law and Harry is Mom's brother. I just talked to Ellen yesterday; she's a friend of my other aunt, Jean, who passed."

"Okay. They're all together."

Several more messages from these lively, talkative spirits come through, all of which Susan validates before her mother resumes her role as primary communicator.

"Your mom says she's happy that you have made progress on going through her belongings. There are so many of these, some very old. She shows newspaper clippings dating to World War II in 1944."

"Yes! The most precious thing I found was a photo album from her wedding. My dad was in the service around 1944, stationed in California, where they got married. There were many newspaper clippings in it. I just thought about that this morning!"

Susan is captivated by the details of what her mother is delivering through me. At this point, I ask if she has any questions. "Ah, yes," she responds. "Could you ask her if there is anything she wants me to do?"

"She wants you to take care of yourself. You see, you've expended a lot of your time and energy taking care of first her and now her estate. She shows me a vacation coming up for you."

Susan grins and then laughs heartily. "Uh-huh. I'm leaving in about 11 days."

"I like to have fun with readings sometimes," I say, joining in on the laughter. Violet is one of the most light-hearted spirits I'd heard from in a long while. In my mind's eye, I see her pointing at her daughter.

"She's saying, 'Get out of here! Go take care of yourself. Go have fun'!"

"That sounds exactly like her."

"She says you look like her, young for your age and pretty."

"Yep, I do. Mom looked 15 or 20 years younger than her age. She was amazing. My birthday was yesterday; I was 64."

"Your mom was ready to cross over. She had congestive heart failure, didn't she?"

"Yes. She was ready; I was the one who wasn't."

"I know. She's so happy over there, dear. She's *so* happy," I convey.

Tears form in Susan's eyes. "Thank you for that."

I am suddenly impressed to share something about my own mother. "You know, when my mom passed over seven years ago, I got a message from her one night. She said, 'Carole, it's more beautiful here than you could ever imagine.' That's what she told me."

"Oh, wow!"

I don't want to lose the link with this spirit so I immediately tune back in. "Your mom says she's come to you through the appearance of cardinals."

"Yes. Just the other day, I was driving and there was a cardinal flying beside me. Two other times when I was driving, one came right by my windshield."

"That's synchronicity. That's your mom's way of saying she's there with you."

The next message Violet gives is peculiar. But, after all, it's not unusual for messages to not make sense (to me) when I hear from the other side. Trusting it *will* make sense to Susan, I give the message.

"She is telling me about Lucille Ball. Do you know why? Was there some connection with that TV show or anything else that you know of?"

Susan looks at me with a blank expression. She gives no validation about this strange message. I instantly feel silly for mentioning it.

In my mind, I ask Violet for clarification, but none is forthcoming. I try to interpret through my intuition. "Did you watch the TV show *I Love Lucy*? Did anyone ever say your hair looks like hers? Do you ever do crazy antics like Lucy did?"

None of these ring a bell with Susan. "I don't know," she replies, shrugging her shoulders.

I decide to table the message. "I don't know why she's showing Lucy. It's really funny that she does, though." I feel the energy from the other side dissipating. "They're starting to pull back. You know, your relatives have come through to me like a party line," I say, laughing.

"I know. My mom and the others were exactly like that-always chatting. I can picture that."

The reading concludes on a light note. "Your mom again says to take care of yourself and have fun!"

Susan thanks me and leaves.

Several months later, she phoned with a startling update about her reading. She asked if I remembered giving her the puzzling message about Lucille Ball. When I replied that I did (because it was so unusual), she excitedly tells me that the day *after* her reading, she received a belated birthday card from her best friend. On the front was a photo of Lucy! Apparently Susan's mother knew about the card before her daughter received it. Energy "chills" crept up the back of my neck as I listened. We were both amazed at the incredible validation her mother had given the day before that card arrived. It was another compelling example of how those in the spirit world are still intricately connected to our lives.

Susan went on to tell me about how her mom's life had affected her.

"My mom was my hero. Over the last year and a half since she passed, I tried to think about what faults she had or what she could have done differently. I couldn't come up with anything. I mean that with all of my heart. She was the kindest person I knew. She taught me how to be caring, and about kindness and generosity. These will always stay with me. My mom's in my heart. I hope I learned enough from her that I can be like her."

The Bright Young Girl

One balmy summer evening, I stepped into the waiting area near my office to greet Denny, who sported a baseball cap and dark sunglasses that obscured his eyes. Two weeks earlier when he called for an appointment, he mysteriously told me that Denny was his middle name and added that if he revealed his first name, I may recognize him. He wanted to keep the reading "pure." I thought this was strange, since I typically don't read for famous people. Although I was curious about whom this man was, I did not discover this until after our session. He kept the hat and glasses on during the entire reading.

I say my prayer and begin. "The first energy who comes through has a similar name to yours on your dad's side. In other words, someone in spirit has the same first or middle name as you. Did you know your ancestors?"

Denny shuffles nervously in his seat for a moment before responding. "My dad's side? Boy, I don't know," he says with a loud sigh. "I don't know much about my family back there."

"Okay. There's a connection with someone with that energy. I feel there's also a legion of people coming through from the other side." Instantly, I am impressed with the distinctive smell of roses. I share this with Denny and ask him to validate what significance roses might have to someone who had passed.

"We did a thing with roses, uh . . ." His voice trails off as he struggles to remember.

"Wait, before you say anything, I must say that I'm being told that there was a tribute of sorts to someone involving roses."

Denny's voice becomes louder as he responds. "Yes, in the past, we did. There were a lot of roses at the tribute."

"I'm seeing a huge amount of roses. The other side is saying they are aware of the tribute. There were a lot of people involved with this. I'm infused with an overwhelming feeling of love. They're using the symbol of the rose to communicate this."

Denny listens intently to everything I am saying and merely shakes his head in agreement.

"Your grandmother on your mom's side- her name starts with

A-N- acts as a spokesperson today in bringing the other energies through."

Again Denny nods but says nothing.

I sense a shift in the spirit communicator who now comes through as a younger woman than the grandmother. "There's a younger feminine energy here. Does that make sense to you?"

"Ah, yeah," Denny says in a barely audible voice. I detect that behind his sunglasses, his eyes are filling with tears. I point to a box of tissues on a nearby table. He rejects my suggestion by waving his hand.

"A first name beginning with K or C is being acknowledged."

Denny chuckles with recognition. "That's my mother, Kathy, who passed."

"Then your mother is the younger energy who is with your grandma." I identify several other spirits who are with her. "There's also the younger female who is with your mom. Do you understand how this is flowing? Here's grandma, your mom and then the younger female. There's a tremendous amount of emotion with this last death. Is this the person who passed quickly?" I am hearing from three spirits and I need Denny to separate them.

"Yes," he answers in a firm voice.

"Is this your daughter?"

"Yes."

"Your mom stresses that your daughter is with her. Your daughter says that she gives signs that she's around you. She also shows me a puppy."

"Well, our dog isn't a puppy anymore."

"No," I insist. "This is a puppy I'm seeing. She makes me feel that someone in the family has a younger dog or is getting a puppy soon."

Denny seems confused. He obviously can't validate the message. I silently ask for clarification. "Just keep the message. Your daughter says she loved animals and is around the dog you have now. Wasn't there something that happened with this dog's ear?"

"Uh, I had an incident in which I felt that the dog heard her."

"I wondered why she is pointing at his ear. Okay. She says your dog is aware of her and you will notice his reaction."

A clairvoyant image forms in my mind. "She shows me the Internet and talks about a tribute to her that's been done." I sense the child-like purity of the young girl as she communicates with us. "She's really excited about that and she is thanking you for creating that page about her. I don't know if this is on Facebook or someplace else. She says that people leave comments on that site. There's also a musical connection to it."

Although I can't see Denny's eyes, I feel his demeanor light up. He sits straight up in his chair and exclaims, "Oh, yeah!"

"She loves the song that you picked. She's saying, 'Dad, I'm really proud of this.' She didn't really know that people thought or felt that way about her."

Denny smiles, sniffles and nods.

The girl continues to pour images and feelings into my mind. "The medallion or necklace that's related to her with an inscription or engraving on it . . . "

My description is interrupted by Denny's reaction. He reaches for the necklace he is wearing and shows it to me.

"Oh, I didn't see that before. She was showing it to me up here," I say, pointing to my head. "She's saying that you wear that a lot or you never take it off. It hangs over your heart. It's a physical remembrance of her, but you know that you will always be connected with her in your spiritual heart."

The next several messages from this vibrant girl concern her soul's lessons. "Your daughter impresses me as a teaching spirit. She was beyond her years spiritually."

"Absolutely," Denny agrees.

"She was here for a short time physically, but her spiritual mission was to present lessons to others. With her passing, there have been a number of challenges for the family to come to terms with. She makes me feel that her death caused issues to come up. Her life and her death touched a lot of people."

Denny moves forward in his chair again. "Yeah!"

"She shows me the ocean. The literal interpretation of that is that someone in the family just went there. The symbolic interpretation is about her life. She can see how her life affected so many people. She makes reference to well-known people; some of them play sports. I hope this makes sense to you."

"My brother just returned from the ocean. Yes, this all makes sense!"

"She shows me autographs and photos—again, some connection with well-known people in sports. Where does the reference to the ball caps with embroidered emblems fit in?" It isn't clear to me what the girl wants me to express.

"I don't know. I never wear caps. I only wore one today so you wouldn't recognize me. We *did* have a number of items made in her memory with embroidery on them."

"Okay then. That's why she mentioned it. She's letting you know that she is aware of the items you made in her memory. Now, there's a connection with you to the West Coast area and also New York," I relay.

"I've been to both of those places since she passed."

The girl infuses me quickly with messages for her dad before he has a chance to validate several of them. "Your daughter comes in with much pride for you. I hear her saying, 'That's my dad!' She also says that you felt that way about her, too. She presents herself as a contemporary to you, a friend. She mentions April as significant for some reason. What happened then?"

Denny searches his memory then responds. "That's when my nephew, my brother's son, passed."

"Oh, dear. You've had such loss at a young age." (Denny appears to be in his late thirties.) At this point, I feel my spirit guides encourage me to make an explanation to Denny.

"You've come in this time to experience transformation. Some of that has not been pleasant but you have made the agreement to deal with a tremendous amount of karma. How you deal with it directly affects your spiritual awareness. By the way, please tell your brother that his son comes through by giving identification of the month he died."

Although he didn't acknowledge it, I get the feeling that the "karmic" explanation hit home with Denny. He simply nods his head and says, "I will definitely tell him."

The communication flows on with the bright girl, who continues to show me images to validate her life. "Your daughter shows me a TV screen and there's a reference to being on TV. This goes to her or to you. She adds that she wants to tell you about the meaning of her life. It was to love people when she was here. She also can't believe how many people loved her. She comes across as humble and extremely beautiful, both physically and spiritually. There's much light that emanates from her soul."

By now, Denny is smiling and crying at the same time. I sense hearing from his daughter brings up a gamut of emotions within him, as it usually does when parents come to hear from their children in sessions.

"You are still processing the physical loss of her and dealing with the emotions from it. But, you know, she stresses that the deeper meaning of her life and death involves helping other people. She delivers a message about some sort of a benefit. It's a big deal."

Denny chuckles. "We just had a huge benefit in her memory!"

"She says she was there. Look at the photos you took."

"That's funny you should say that. In one of them, when the pastor was giving the blessing, there's a white, circular light that appears in the background between him and me. We don't know what it is."

"Yes, that's why she said she was there. It's an orb, evidence of a spiritual presence. She also says that October means something special to her."

"I don't know," Denny replies. "I'll probably think of these things once I leave here. I just wanted to make sure she was okay. I do believe our spiritual self lives on after death."

I knew due to the validations of other readings I've done that Denny would be able to confirm messages later. "Of course, I can assure you we do live on. The short time your daughter was here, she made a huge impact on people. She continues to do that with an even greater impact *after* her death. This is through the positive ways her life will affect people. Her life and death have taught people about generosity, compassion and understanding. Her life was that significant. You know, she's a very advanced soul."

"Yeah, she was and continues to be an amazing girl."

"She was not only a teacher, but a healer through you. She shows an image of you standing up in front of people and speaking. She is right behind you, inspiring you. She says that you've talked to young people to make them aware of what they're doing, not doing and to value their lives."

"Yes, I've done that many times."

"One other thing comes up from her. She mentions Virginia or the Washington, DC area. She shows you going there for some reason."

Denny is unable to validate the message so I suggest that he file it and see what happens later.

At the close of the reading, Denny removes his "disguise" and tells me his real name. I don't recognize him and wonder why he wanted to remain anonymous during the reading. He shares with me that his daughter had been brutally murdered by an ex-boyfriend the day after her 16th birthday. Since that time, he had appeared on several national TV shows to speak about the issue of date violence for young people. He wore the hat and sunglasses because he was concerned I might recognize him from TV. As a result of his daughter's tragic death, he has been instrumental in getting state legislation passed that endorses education about teen dating violence in high schools.

A month after the reading, Denny told me about an astounding validation of the Washington trip his daughter mentioned in the reading. Two weeks after the session, he and three other families who had also lost children were invited to the home of Vice President Joe Biden in the District of Columbia to discuss their efforts to end violence and abuse against young people. At the time of the reading, Denny had no knowledge of the trip, yet his daughter in spirit did. Further, he confirmed that October 6 is the date approved by the Pennsylvania state legislature in memory of his daughter. I explained that these validations give reassurance that his daughter knows about these events related to her life.

"My daughter's death has been so painful that if I didn't do advocacy, the pain would eat me alive," he shares. "I speak to groups of young people to help them avoid what happened to her and also to honor her. My daughter means everything to me. She taught me about unconditional love. Life is short. Her life has revealed to me that our time here really does matter."

PART THREE:

THE LIGHT WITHIN YOU

Nine

Moving Beyond the Realm of Thought

God, whose love is everywhere, can't come to visit unless you're not there.
Angelus Silesius

The above quote by a 16th Century philosopher and mystic cleverly describes how our personality and ego—aspects of our conscious, rational mind—can obscure our awareness of the intuitive, divine intelligence within. This spiritual dimension is ever present, accessible and fresh, regardless of the life circumstances that seem to temporarily diminish its light from our consciousness. It is the unchangeable essence within each human being that has existed since the beginning of creation and will survive eternally. It manifests itself moment by moment, fully independent of the past and future.

Many people become so identified with their thoughts and emotions that they are oblivious to the magnitude of the spiritual presence that radiates from the core of their being. Thoughts and emotions such as fear, anger, hatred, resentment, jealousy, anxiety and misunderstanding take root and proliferate in the domain of the ego and personality. Eventually, these negative states of mind create needless suffering because they deny the spiritual core within us and reinforce the belief that we are separate from others.

One look at the state of the world today reveals the horror that results from ignoring our spiritual identity, the unity we share with one another, animals and the earth. Why is this so? More importantly, how can we transform it? If we cannot heal ourselves, how can we expect to make the world a better place?

The answer begins and ends with our awakening to our spiritual essence and listening to the voice of our own soul. Healing relationships with others necessitates that we first heal ourselves by acknowledging the radiance of our own spiritual light, which obliterates the darkness of painful, ego-centered thoughts and emotions.

How do we become aware of this light within us and how do we nurture it? The conscious mind is preoccupied with thinking and its conceptual reality focuses on linear concepts such as time, space and reasoning. The soul as the inexhaustible essence of the Divine within each individual exists beyond these mental constructs. When becoming aware of this eternal core of ourselves, we must go beyond the rational mind by stilling it. Then and only then can we move beyond the realm of thought that keeps us shackled to our personality and ego.

Meditation and Stillness Create and Sustain Awareness of Spirit

If you have already embarked on your spiritual journey, you know how relevant meditation is to the process of awakening to Spirit within. If you have not, I encourage you to read this section several times. Then, put the book down and become still. I promise you won't be disappointed with what you experience, unless you harbor expectations about what *should* happen during your still time.

For example, you may think that you *should* see, hear or sense something or someone during meditation. Or you may believe you will magically be transported to another place or time. In all the years I've been meditating, this has happened to me only a few times. As you've read in earlier chapters, expectations can severely diminish the connection we make with Spirit. So it's best to release your notions about what should happen during meditation. Becoming still is simply becoming mindful of who you are beyond your mind and personality.

Meditation is the process of going within oneself to become aware of the divine life force. As such, it requires that the conscious mind be quieted so that we can become aware of this inner essence. Stillness is just that: we enter into a state of being that is conducive to our receiving this awareness. Since healing means that we reawaken to our pure divinity, it necessitates that we become aware of that essence. We can become still in virtually any physical setting by focusing on the presence of Spirit within. As you'll see, this is easily done by accessing your own breath.

Some people are intimidated by the thought of meditating. Personally, I believe this is due to inaccurate perceptions about what meditation is and how simply it can be accomplished. In some cases, people fear becoming quiet because they are addicted to the constant stream of thoughts that consume their daily awareness. They are distrustful of what they perceive as "emptiness." The good news is that this resistance can be overcome and those who have no experience with meditation can quickly and easily reach beyond their conscious mind by using simple, readily available techniques.

Simple Breath and Body Awareness Techniques for Stillness

The most common obstacle that most people struggle with when they begin to meditate is the perceived inability to quiet the mind. When I teach spiritual development workshops, this topic invariably comes up. Often, people become frustrated and discouraged when their thoughts interrupt or dominate the silent state of meditation. Then they give up, declaring they can't do it, defeated by their own thoughts. This is a form of self-sabotage and the ego's way of staying in control. To avoid falling into this trap, you must first be aware of it. That's why I'm mentioning it here.

I've discovered on my personal spiritual journey that simple, direct methods of connecting with Spirit are the best. Long, complicated meditations done in uncomfortable postures do not work for me. They never have and probably never will. I've discovered that since Spirit within is as close as my breath, I can use the simple action of breathing to access it. The intent of meditation is to feel the spiritual core of one's being beyond the realm of thinking. The breath—ever present and in the moment—is a convenient vehicle of transport to connect with the inner awareness of being. This exercise can be done anywhere, anytime, without props such as music, pillows or candles.

To go within using your breath, close your eyes (except if you are driving or require alertness in any way) and notice the rise and fall of your chest as you breathe. Follow your breath with your awareness as it goes in and out of your body. If you'd like, imagine the breath restoring perfect balance to each cell of your body. In a few moments, you will notice the calm awareness that lies beneath your thoughts. When you are ready, open your eyes to normal, waking consciousness. That's it. You can do this as many times throughout the day as you want. This exercise is particularly helpful in times of stress, fatigue or emotional upset because it restores your attention to the dimension that lies beyond these physical states. It can be done during the course of a work day, in the morning or at night. It works because it diverts attention away from thinking into present moment awareness.

Another technique to connect inwardly is through creating body awareness. Start with the above breath awareness exercise. Once you are still, focus your attention on various areas of your body. Start with your hands and then move to your torso, your legs and your feet. Feel and observe the flow of Spirit in these areas of your body. Like breath awareness, focusing attention on the body interrupts identification with thought.

Remember that the purpose of both of these exercises is to touch the essence of Spirit within, not to completely shut out your thoughts. In fact, most people (even those who are experienced in meditation) cannot completely turn off their thoughts. The following imagery will help you when thoughts begin to bombard your stillness:

Imagine that you are in a garden lying on the soft grass, looking up at the sky. When a thought comes into your mind during periods of stillness, see the thought as a cloud, calmly drifting over you. Observe it as it passes over you and moves on. Realize it has no effect on you, the observer. Watch it as it passes over you. Then refocus on your breath. If another thought comes, do the same, refocusing on your breath.

By simply observing your thoughts, you allow them to come and go without becoming attached to them. You simply notice them instead of allowing them to control you.

Reducing Drifting, Mind Chatter and Lack of Trust

When I began spiritual practice years ago, I was amazed at how good I felt during and after meditation. This continued for a while and then problems began to arise. In those days, my meditations often lasted an hour or so daily. Soon, I found myself drifting and becoming bored. During quiet time, my mind obsessed about what I could or should be doing that was more productive. The stillness seemed like a waste of time. After all, I had other things to do. How could I justify an hour of doing nothing? My mind zoomed on and on, with one excuse after another about what I needed to be doing. Soon after, I began to distrust the connection I was supposedly making with Spirit. How did I know that what I was feeling during mediation was real? When I did receive guidance, how could I validate its accuracy? Maybe I was making it all up from wishful thinking.

In the midst of this confusion, I received an intuitive wake-up call from one of my spirit guides: *Carole, if you're going to go into meditation with such a negative attitude, you may as well not do it at all. Go do something else. In the future, shorten your meditations so you do not drift or become bored. Over and out…*

Okay, I thought, *maybe my guide has something here.* I decided to test this new advice. From that day forward, I began meditating for about five minutes per session, several times a day. Since then, I've successfully eliminated most drifting. I still deal with mind chatter but I don't let it control me. Developing trust took a little longer. I soon realized that my mind wanted to dominate my experience of meditating by trying to impose its rigid structure on the formless flow of Spirit. I reasoned that this was due to the fear of somehow losing control. I needed to give my mind permission to let go, one moment at a time. To help with this, I used breath awareness and guided imagery (see the meditation at the end of this chapter.) Little by little, I merged with stillness instead of resisting it.

If you find yourself dealing with the obstacles of drifting, mind chatter and lack of trust in the process of going within, I assure you that they don't have to stop you from feeling Spirit within. They have only the power that you give them. Connecting with your spiritual essence transcends the limitations of your mind. Above all, don't give up! Remember that it is not possible to "fail" at meditation because as long as you're breathing, you can successfully meditate through stillness.

Acceptance is Healing

As I mention in earlier chapters, all healing begins through the recognition of oneself as Spirit—right here, right now, in the present moment. We are not victims or prisoners of the past except through the thoughts generated by our own minds, where that illusion exists. That is why present time awareness— available through meditation and stillness—is fundamental to healing. It pulls our focus to the only available power point there is: the moment. Going beyond the rational mind is freeing because it liberates us from the artificial constructs of time, form and thought. This, in turn, moves us away from resistance to life's circumstances and toward acceptance of them. Becoming aware of Spirit within is like taking a deep breath, letting it go and becoming totally relaxed. It's little wonder that the breath is an effective, convenient vehicle to reach this inner presence.

Nearly 29 years ago, I entered into a 12 step recovery program. These steps are the suggested core guidelines in obtaining and maintaining sobriety. In the recovery groups that I attended, I learned that sobriety was not necessarily guaranteed by following the steps, but that I had a much better chance at it by "working" each step to the best of my ability, one day at a time. By this point, I knew that what I had been doing with my life prior to entering the program wasn't working. I was at the end of the rope, so to speak. Undeniably, I had to chart another course. So I read and reread the steps in the program pamphlets. I listened to them read aloud and discussed them at dozens of meetings. They emphasized the necessity of becoming aware of a "Higher Power" that would heal me from the disease of addiction. This power did not have to be God according to the tenets of organized religion, but a God of *my* understanding. The single, inescapable requirement was that the power be something greater than myself (my own ego), which had led me into addiction from the beginning. The first step in developing awareness of this Higher Power was accepting that I was powerless over alcohol and that my life had become unmanageable. I soon realized that it would be impossible for me to stay sober without anchoring the awareness of the Higher Power within me.

Some time ago, it occurred to me (and others I've spoken with) that the 12 steps used in recovery from substances can also be applied to the process of spiritual awakening and to healing specific life issues. The key concepts of each original step are the same, regardless of the issue involved. For our purposes here, I've chosen to discuss several of these as they relate to developing spiritual consciousness and healing relationships. (To read all of the steps or learn about 12 step recovery, see Recommended Resources.)

Surrendering to a Higher Power within implies that we accept the fact that we cannot control others or the external events in our life from the standpoint of our own personal will. It means giving up resistance (the ego's domain) to what we are experiencing at any given moment. We admit to ourselves that our attempts to heal our life and relationships have not been successful. This step requires trust, humility, courage and honesty. Taking this crucial first step brings us squarely into *acceptance*, which ends personal resistance to the situation. Initially, our ego perceives surrender as a loss of personal power or weakness when, in truth, the only genuine power we ever possess resides in the unwavering presence of Spirit within. From this higher vantage point, we relinquish our need to control the situation, from our own ego's limited perspective, which often results in suffering. We can now understand how our previous thoughts- emanating from our mind as an extension of the ego-were futile in finding peace and resolution.

In the years that I attended 12-step recovery groups, I heard the phrase "Let go and let God" repeated countless times. In some meetings, it was printed on bumper stickers that were available for purchase. This simple phrase addresses the importance of surrendering the ego's relentless need to control the outcome of situations, other people and life, generally speaking.

In healing relationships with those in spirit, we must release outworn, self-defeating emotions such as guilt, shame, anger and resentment that have kept our hearts imprisoned. We are no longer victimized by our thoughts and feelings when we view them as the teaching vehicles for spiritual understanding that they are. Letting go of them opens the door to true forgiveness, the foundation for healing. Honesty is required since we can no longer deny or impose expectations on the reality of the situation we face, if we truly accept it as it is. This takes courage and conviction. Admitting that we are powerless over everyone and everything outside of ourselves can be difficult because we must let go of our old way of thinking without yet knowing where life will lead us. We might ask, "What now?" That is where the next step comes in: We become aware that peace and freedom from suffering come from believing in a power greater than our own ego- the Higher Self or Spirit within.

The Higher Self Brings Freedom

Recognizing and accepting that there is something beyond our human ego enables us to transcend it. Just as humility, honesty and surrender are intrinsic to taking the first step, the second requires trust on our behalf until *believing* in a power greater than oneself transforms into *knowing* there is a force beyond the ego. Eventually, we become aware that this power lies within us, not outside.

In the process of spiritual awakening, the words "Higher Self" can easily be substituted for "Higher Power." Both refer to the eternal, flowing divine essence that resides within us. Awareness of the Higher Self liberates us from the structured enclosures of the mind and ego. Becoming aware of our divine identity (beyond the past conditioning of our minds) creates awareness that we are not limited, controlled or diminished by these unbalanced thoughts and feelings. Our real, true self exists independently from them.

Spiritual awakening and healing occur when detachment from our ego becomes the means by which we can rise above it. In order to do this, we must learn to observe life without investing the ego in the process, since it has been the source of our suffering. This especially applies to relationships in which others frequently mirror our own unresolved mental and emotional states. Knowing that we no longer have to be trapped in the limited dimensions of our own mind to navigate through life, we experience the joys of true freedom.

Forgive Everyone (Including Yourself) All the Time

In early recovery, I learned that the act of forgiveness was paramount to the maintenance of my sobriety. In my study of the 12 steps and their application to my life, I discovered that the core teaching of steps four through 10 focuses on forgiveness of both self and others. The concept of "letting go" surfaced again and again the longer I stayed sober. *What exactly did I need to let go of?* I wondered. The answer revealed itself as I continued to work the steps: anyone, anything and everything that I (my ego) might use as "ammunition" or excuses to drink again. These things primarily concerned my own thoughts and emotions, not those of others. So, I went about the business of engaging in self-forgiveness by writing about what I needed to change within myself. I wrote a long list. After a short time, I humbly asked Spirit through prayer to remove these unhealed thoughts. Day by day, my life slowly got better.

When we want to heal a relationship with another, we must become willing to let go of the past. Once we accept the truth of the situaion, we need to let go of it through forgiveness. In Chapter One, I stress the relevance of forgiveness to healing. Carrying the burdens of the past negatively impacts our ability to be in the present moment, the birthplace of healing. Forgiveness enables us to move beyond the past into present time awareness.

Many people forget to forgive themselves when healing relationships. Contrary to believing that we are perfectly (falsely) justified in our feelings or actions towards others is the thought that we are guilty of perceived wrongdoings towards others. These negative thoughts become the proverbial thorns in our sides and form the basis for self-inflicted emotional punishment. Left unhealed, they could potentially contribute to the development of physical and emotional illnesses. As you read in Chapters Six and Seven, people can harbor unresolved emotions for years before realizing that forgiveness frees them from doing so. In the truth of Spirit, we are always guiltless, no matter what the circumstance. To grasp that concept, we might say that we (or others) experienced a circumstance or relationship according to the mindset or consciousness we had at the time. Ultimately, all life's experiences lead to our soul's evolution and are therefore inherently good in a spiritual sense.

In my personal spiritual journey, I've found that daily forgiveness of myself and others is not only beneficial to spiritual growth, it is absolutely necessary because it eliminates the burden of negative thoughts from my consciousness. In my commitment to being aware of my Higher Self, forgiveness ensures that I do not become entangled in misguided thoughts and feelings. To clear these, I've used the following exercise, which you, too, may find helpful:

Go into a quiet space. Close your eyes and focus on your breath, allowing it to pull you inward. Now focus on your heart. Imagine that the breath is opening your heart to its fullest capacity to give and receive love, compassion and forgiveness.

Invite your Higher Self and Spirit to be with you in the moment. If you have a particular image of the Divine (Jesus, Buddha, Krishna, for example), see that image in your mind's eye. Feel this loving Presence within you. Ask that Spirit be with you, healing you from the past and all perceived wrongs that you or others have done. Silently or out loud, name those people, seeing them as clearly as you can in your mind's eye. If you are doing self-forgiveness, see yourself. Now see yourself and the others encompassed by golden light. Silently or out loud, say, "You are free. I am free. I release you in forgiveness and through the purity of Spirit. And so it is."

Take a deep breath and give thanks to your Higher Self and Spirit. Open your eyes and relax.

Engaging in this easy exercise daily will help keep your slate clean by clearing away the debris from your heart and soul.

Merging Our Will with Divine Will Leads to Successful Living

When I was working the program of recovery, it became necessary to infiltrate my conscious mind and will with the awareness of my Higher Self through using the spiritual tools of prayer and meditation. In spiritual development and healing, engaging in these states of awareness gives direct access to Spirit. They amplify the voice within that intuitively knows what we need, often before our rational mind becomes aware of it. The still states of prayer and meditation merge the formless energy of Spirit with the physical mind.

When applying this step, it's important to distinguish the difference between mental knowledge and intuitive knowing. The rational left brain gathers, perceives and stores information through the use of the five physical senses. It then interprets the information according to structured thought patterns, most of which have been formed by its own or others' prior experiences. To the conscious mind, information must be proven by logic or through physical data before it is accepted as valid. To the contrary, the intuitive right brain *senses* information, which is received through the inner senses. The information may or may not be substantiated by prior experiences or through physical means. Meditation and prayer are gateways that open the intuitive mind, the seat of the Higher Self. Balanced, harmonious living requires the infusion of the Divine (the intuitive mind) with the rational mind.

How often do we struggle with knowing exactly what to do in a particular situation? In many sessions I've done, people want to know how to go about healing seemingly irreparable rifts with family or friends, both living and deceased. Approaching the situation from using only their ego (rational mind) has brought everyone involved more frustration, anger and pain. In most cases, people lose hope and shut down. Life becomes difficult and heavy. The solution is to initiate communication with the Higher Self in the intuitive mind and to trust the guidance that it gives. If we are an open channel for its messages and promptings, we will always do the right thing at the right time. Sometimes that guidance will not make sense to our rational minds and that is why it's best to ask for the power to carry it out, despite our resistance. The reward of healing results from our letting go of our will and being open to intuitively sensing divine will. That is authentic power, not the illusion of power the ego generates.

As someone who practices metaphysical spirituality, I've been asked why certain events happen and why they occur in the timing that they do. Earlier, I explained that the soul operates with its own sense of divine timing and how that timing affects its transition into the spirit world. This same divine timing applies to the soul as it expresses itself in the physical world. If we ignore this innate wisdom, we are forced (by default) to operate within the limited framework of our mind, ego and personality. That is where we get into trouble and problems are compounded. Situations appear overwhelming and insur-mountable. Following intuitive guidance always puts us where we need to be for the highest, most beneficial evolution of our soul.

Guidance from the Higher Self revealed through prayer and meditation illuminates the pathway to the heart. Merging our human will with divine will means that we use our minds, egos and personalities to act on this higher guidance. We act in accor-dance with the Higher Self instead of reacting from the person-ality. At times, the direction we receive is consistent with what we already believed to be true and other times it is not. It's helpful to remember that we are seldom given guidance that we do not have the strength to act on. The only real obstacle is our own stubborn will, encased in a rigid belief system.

Not long ago, I was drawn into a discussion about my beliefs on reincarnation and free will with Frank, an acquaintance from the gym I visit regularly. I was hesitant to engage in conversation with him because I immediately sensed anger in his demeanor. But since he seemed eager to initiate the conversation, I quietly shared with him about my experiences of seeing past-life scenarios and karma around people in numerous sessions I'd done. Just as I had felt, he quickly and flatly rejected the concept of karma by saying that his father in spirit was doomed to be an s.o.b. (his words) from the time he was born. According to Frank, there was no such thing as free will or choice, only fate. He went on to reveal that his father had been extremely abusive to him and that their relationship had never been healed before he passed. It was definitely a no-win situation as far as he was concerned.

As the conversation progressed, I felt Frank's resistance escalate when I suggested that he try to understand his father from a different perspective—namely, that his father had probably never had a spiritual awareness in life which accounted for his lack of love. Again he rejected the idea, which I sensed he found threatening. There was simply no "excuse" for why his father had been so mean-spirited. I chose to end the conversation since Frank's ego was so strongly invested in the discussion. Clearly, it was pointless to try to change Frank's mind since he wasn't able to get beyond his own rigid beliefs. But the encounter reinforced and validated my own spiritual growth, namely, the need to release judgment about anyone's spiritual beliefs or life experiences.

The power to carry out divine will implies that we must get out of our own way, as far as our ego is concerned. It means that we no longer take unpleasant life circumstances personally. Trusting that Spirit is always leading us towards continued evolution of our soul is the sure-fire pathway to healing and spiritual awakening.

Living in Spirit

About five years into recovery, I offer you my personal validation that I experienced a spiritual awakening, as promised in the 12th step. My life was radically, positively better than before I started. I had spoken at various 12-step groups about my life before and after self-medicating with alcohol. I prayed daily and attended many discussion meetings to absorb the wisdom of the long-time members and to help newcomers. I felt vigorously alive and profoundly free. Life itself had not changed; my attitude towards it had. Day by day, I found myself living in the light of my authentic being, not in the darkness of my former imprisoned self. I cannot say if the 12-step program saved my physical life as others have claimed, but I can attest that it was fundamental to a remarkable spiritual awakening. The pathway I am on today is the result of opening my heart to the honesty, willingness and strength of Spirit.

Practicing the core principles of the program simply means using them every day. Connecting with the Higher Self through prayer and meditation, and engaging in forgiveness are the keynotes of harmonious living. Going to Spirit first when challenges arise removes ego from the process. Although this doesn't automatically guarantee immediate success in resolving problems, we are much more likely to avoid pain and unhappiness in the interim. Impatience and frustration lessen if we place our confidence in Spirit as the journey unfolds.

How can we bring the light we've found within ourselves to others? By *being* that light. In the years I've done readings, I've met people from all walks of life who beautifully radiate the light of divine consciousness, despite personal hardship or tragedy. A striking example is Barbara, who lost 22-year-old Julie, her only child. Initially immersed in heart-wrenching grief after Julie passed, Barbara questioned how such a tragedy could happen. Was God punishing her by taking her only child? How could a loving God do such a thing? After awhile, she transformed her grief into service by becoming actively involved in the same civic organization Julie that had been a member of- a group that helped veterans. The last time we spoke, she shared her experiences about volunteering with the organization, which had memorialized Julie for her past dedication. Despite her pain, Barbara was not afraid to be the light for others who needed her. She did not wallow in grief or anger. The message she carries to others is one that illuminates the divine qualities of strength, hope and compassion.

My message to you is that if you feel lost, alone, depressed or fearful, know that Spirit has not neglected or abandoned you. This very moment is where the absolute power of your soul resides. All you need is already within you, waiting patiently for you to awaken to its glorious reality. Of that, you can be certain.

Moving Comfortably Between Thinking and Being

From the time I began my spiritual journey, I've been learning how to integrate my personality with the awareness of myself as Spirit. I refer to these as "little me" and "big me," respectively. Over time and with daily practice, merging the two has become easier. Before each reading, I meditate to connect with the "big me," Spirit within. Then I pray by asking for the highest and best experience and guidance for my client. Using both tools helps to clear any interference or static from my rational mind, the seat of my personality. These practices have become so much a part of my everyday living that I feel disoriented if I occasionally don't have the opportunity to do them.

In the early stages of my spiritual awakening, I hungrily read countless books about metaphysical topics, as if I could not absorb enough knowledge about spiritual topics. I would then discuss what I had read with others who were open to the same pathway. I was consumed with *knowing* about Spirit but had little direct experience of it in those days. Eventually I began to feel hollow and unfulfilled. In the last five years or so, I've slowly turned away from accumulating knowledge by recognizing my desire to develop a personal relationship with Spirit. Today, I am much more centered in my spiritual awareness by feeding both my mind and soul. For me, a direct experience of the divine essence within is absolutely indispensible because I have discovered that I will never "know" it through my mind.

Living a heart-centered, spiritually awakened life does not imply ignoring that we are human beings with physical bodies and rational minds. Nor does it mean that we live in seclusion, without interacting with others, meditating and praying day and night. It is far more realistic to become spiritually aware using a balanced approach that blends still states (meditation, prayer, yoga) with active ones (reading, taking workshops, volunteering, discussion groups.) Becoming overly dependent on any state may actually be more detrimental than having no awareness at all if it is used as a form of escape. Relying on the perspective of the rational mind alone or continually removing ourselves from the physical world by shutting it out does not support rewarding, harmonious living. Both are unhealthy attachments that will eventually lead to isolation and unhappiness.

To move comfortably between thinking and being, practice going in and out of short meditations frequently. The breath-awareness focus exercise is an easy way for you to do this anytime, anywhere. This merges the unconscious flow of Spirit with your conscious mind. You can also still your rational mind by silently observing nature. Open to the essence of Spirit that is within a plant, tree, flower or animal that you are observing. At the same time you observe, focus on your breath. Realize that the same energy that is present in your breath flows through nature. Notice that rational thinking stops when you focus your awareness beyond your mind. Then, when you are ready, bring your awareness back to whatever you were doing or thinking before the break.

I have frequently been on what I refer to as the "treadmill" —

repetitive, persistent thoughts generated by my mind. At times, it seems that the harder I try to calm my mind using rational thought alone, the louder the thoughts become. For instance, I might think, *Release those thoughts!* or *It's ridiculous to believe that!* only to have them become more intense. Instead of using thought against thought, I've found the best way to get off of the treadmill is to move beyond it by shifting my focus inward using my breath or body awareness. I've discovered that if I judge the thoughts I am having, they grow in proportion. So I merely observe them and direct my attention inward. One thing is certain: I will probably be back on the treadmill at some point but I won't allow it to coerce me into believing those thoughts from the "little me" have power over the "big me."

The rational mind is concerned with distinct beginnings and endings, whereas the Higher Self circulates endlessly. Try this: the next time you are engaged in an activity (especially one that you find routine or dull), see if you can remove thinking from it and be in the flow of the process. Go into the timeless awareness within. If it is an activity that you don't like to do, go within, using your breath, while doing it. You will soon feel more enthusiasm and appreciation during the process.

Moving comfortably between thinking and being promotes harmony within yourself because it validates the reality of your spiritual core. Becoming conscious of Spirit in everyday life brings vibrant awareness to what was formerly mundane or challenging. Work becomes pleasurable. Perceived losses in life are overcome. The past becomes insignificant in defining who you are in the present. You are empowered.

Meditations to Move Beyond the Realm of Thought

These meditations will help you access the Divine within. They can be used for self- healing, forgiveness, connection with loved ones in spirit or for relaxation. Before doing them, choose a quiet environment, away from distractions. You can light a candle and sit or lie on a pillow. Of course, don't do them while driving since you will be closing your eyes. Do not be discouraged or concerned if you do not see any images or hear anything during meditation. Open your heart to receive the experiences that come your way. The most important thing is that you become still and open to Spirit.

You are the Rose:

This meditation leads you into your heart, the seat of the Divine, through simple visualizations. If you'd like, place a fresh rose nearby and smell its fragrance before and after the meditation.

Relax and focus on your breath, and allow it to pull you inward. Focus on your breath as it circulates through your body. Become aware of your hands, abdomen and feet. Bring your awareness into your heart. Feel and visualize the breath enter your heart. Imagine that your physical heart is cleansed and renewed with each breath, which appears as a golden stream of light, pouring down from above your head.

Now, gently go into the depth of emotions in your heart. What feelings come up? If they are uncomfortable or unpleasant, simply observe them. Perhaps they are associated with a person or event in your life. Observe who or what is connected to the feeling. Now imagine that the stream of light washes away feelings of unforgiveness, pain, resentment, bitterness or anger. You are free and perfect right here, right now. Take a deep breath.

As you stay in this soothing energy, see the form of a beautiful rose slowly appear in the center of your heart. It does not matter what color the rose is. Allow it to be in whatever way it comes to you. See the rose open, petal by petal. As each petal unfolds, the innate perfection of the rose is revealed to you. See, sense and smell it. Imagine its velvety petals are touching your fingertips. Feel the aliveness in each petal. Each atom is alive with an innate order, harmony and perfection. Imagine that the rose is your heart, opening to its full capacity to give and receive love.

In your mind's eye, look deeply into the center of the rose. What do you sense? Merge your awareness with the rose by continuing to focus on the center of it. Feel its beauty and vitality within you. Place your hand on your heart and feel this same sacred presence within your own being. The divine presence in you is fully awake and alive now, unencumbered by the past. Breathe deeply and relax.

Now open your eyes and return to full waking consciousness.

The Purifying Flame for Inner Transformation:

Each day, we exchange energy with the outer world through the energy circuits connected to our body. Because these circuits can become clogged with excess or unwanted energetic "baggage," they should be cleansed daily to maintain health and well being, just like the physical body. The following meditation is a simple way to do this. It can be done at night before sleep, or in the morning before starting your day.

Relax and focus on your breath. Allow the breath to direct your attention inward. Feel it circulate throughout your physical body. Feel the presence of your hands, feet and abdomen. Next, imagine that a brilliant, purple-colored flame appears at the top of your head. This healing flame will burn away all impurities in your energy circuits and restore perfect balance to your mind, emotions and body. What remains will be the pure essence of the Divine within you.

As you continue to observe it, the flame encircles your entire body, from head to toe. See the bright flame extending outward and away from your body as it burns. Feel it purify your body. Stay with the visualization for a few moments. Now take a deep breath and affirm, "I am radiant, whole and free. My divine, perfect self is all there is. I am at peace."

A Visit to the Garden of Beloved Souls:

This meditation is designed to strengthen and heal your relationships with loved ones in spirit. In preparation, you may want to have photos of your loved ones nearby, and you may wish to light a candle. If you intend to use the meditation for healing, it's helpful to write down specifically what you want to release.

Then write what you would like to bring into your awareness. For example: "I am releasing the emotional pain of feeling unloved by my mother. I now love and nurture myself unconditionally." During the meditation, it's best to release all expectations about the experience you will have and go inward with an open heart.

Begin by focusing on your breath. Allow it to lead you within. If, at any time during the meditation thoughts distract you, refocus your attention on your breath. After a few moments, place your attention on your heart, feeling the breath open this energy center to its fullest capacity. Breathe deeply. Affirm "I give and receive love freely and without limitations. I live and breathe in love."

Invite loved ones in spirit to be with you. Welcome them into your heart. In your mind's eye, see their faces and look deeply into their eyes. Feel their presence with you now.

Walk together on a pathway through a vibrantly green meadow to a fresh, colorful summer garden. Atop the ornate gate at the entrance are the words "Garden of Beloved Souls." Once inside the gates, you see hummingbirds, butterflies and bees flutter around many brightly-colored flowers in full bloom. Sparkling, blue water flows from a towering fountain in the center of the garden. You are in awe of the beauty of this place. As you move further along the pathway into the garden, the air becomes light and sweet with fragrance. Peace encompasses you. In the stillness, you are cradled in serenity.

In the tranquility of the garden, you are deeply connected to those in spirit. See the light emanating from their souls. In turn, they acknowledge your light. In this silent sharing, the past is nonexistent. There is only this perfect moment. If there has been pain or challenge in your relationships, bring those to the sacred garden to be released. If you do not have the willingness to forgive, ask Spirit for it. Remember to also forgive yourself, as well as others. In this moment, it is done. Breathe deeply and release.

Before leaving the garden, give thanks for the experience you have had here today. Express gratitude for all of your relationships.

Acknowledge that health, abundance and healing are here for you now. Now open your eyes, breathe deeply and stretch. If you'd like, you can record your experiences in your journal. Peace is with you.

The Real You

Recently, I had a compelling experience that led me to connect more deeply with the spiritual presence within myself. After suffering unexplained debilitating muscle and joint pain for two months, I was finally diagnosed with an auto-immune illness. Until this condition manifested, I had enjoyed good health. I rarely took over-the-counter medications, exercised regularly and took natural daily supplements. Overnight, my life changed. I could barely get out of bed in the morning due to pain and stiffness in my shoulders, hands, toes and jaw. Routine tasks such as showering, walking and writing became challenging, to say the least. Aspirin and other pain relievers offered little relief. I was angry and scared. One morning before I had received a diagnosis, the pain was particularly intense. I lay in bed and thought, *Am I the same person who lifted weights in the gym three times a week and barely took a break from work? Where is that person now? She has suddenly vanished. I can barely lift my arms. Who am I beyond my body and this pain?*

In that moment, it dawned on me that my awareness was still intact, evidenced by the fact that I could observe what was happening to my body. I was greatly comforted by realizing that the pain was happening *to* me, but was *not* me. The core essence, the real me, was beyond my physical body. Over and over in my head, I said, *This too, shall pass.* Still I obsessed about how or why this was happening to me.

Six months of treatment with medication has gradually brought the condition into remission. At this point, I'm grateful for the wake-up call that the illness has brought me. I was literally forced by my physical condition to look within myself for the *real* me- the essence that exists beyond pain, thought, emotion and the physical body. Paradoxically, my body was the same vehicle through which this essence made itself known. Through the months, my awareness gradually shifted from victimhood into acceptance. I am appreciative of the sanctity of my life and substantially more understanding of the need to detach from identification with my physical body. Because my mobility was temporarily restricted, I focused much more on "being" than "doing," which was a significant transformation for me. The illness may have been the only way my Higher Self could get me to shift my focus to stillness.

The true essence of who you are lies beyond the realm of your mind, thoughts, emotions and body. As you shift your awareness to discover your real self, you are positively transformed forever. The door closes on the ego-self when you befriend the shining light within. Who you *thought* you were dissolves and gives way to the experience of self as Spirit. You flow with life instead of resisting it. Various wake-up calls in life may point you towards the greater reality of who you are, but it is ultimately up to you to pay attention to them.

An undeniable truth that I have learned from communicating with the spirit world is that we will take only love and service with us when we die. Everything else will be left behind. Countless souls who have come through in readings have delivered messages to surviving family and friends about taking the rewards of these two precious commodities with them upon passing. It is certainly true that the level of spiritual consciousness we have in life determines where we will go after death and how our soul will continue to evolve once there. As we continue on the pathway that will invariably lead us back home to the spirit world, our quality of life in the physical dimension is solely our responsibility. Recognizing ourselves as the embodiment of the one, eternal Spirit is where the journey begins and ends.

Ten

Creating Spiritual Intimacy

Likewise the Spirit helps us in our weakness . . .
that very Spirit intercedes with sighs too deep for words.
Romans 8:26

As you dedicate yourself to walking the path of Spirit, you will continue to awaken to the truth of who you are apart from the mask of your personality and ego. During this journey, you may wonder how you can heighten and sustain a connection with your higher awareness. What do you do if you feel "blocked?" After the initial "high" of deeper self- discovery wears off, how can you continue to cultivate spiritual growth, especially during periods of stress, change, fear or crisis?

In the last decade, people have asked me to teach them how to open, trust and maintain spiritual awareness, as well as how to connect with loved ones in spirit. In my workshops, I've met with and supported people from all walks of life in finding their unique pathway to spiritual self-discovery through developing their intuition. In this chapter, I present you with the highlights of many hours of that intuitive development training.

I'd like to point out that this information is not necessarily intended for you to become a professional psychic or medium, although I make references about sensing and reading energy. (I assure you that if psychic mediumship is your calling in life, it will undoubtedly find you.) Rather, the material I present here highlights simple, practical methods gleaned from my personal and professional experience that anyone can use to open and trust intuition. Since I've been asked frequently to help people make their own connection to loved ones in spirit, I offer techniques that I have personally and successfully used in the development of mediumship. I share these guidelines with my sincere wish for the highest and best experience on your sacred pathway. There are myriad pathways that lead home to Spirit; I encourage you to make use of what feels the most natural in your personal development.

Discover Spirit by Listening to Your Intuition

As I've mentioned numerous times, every human being contains the perfect seed of the Divine within; I have referred to this consciousness as the Higher Self. No matter what it is called, this essence is present and vibrantly alive within us in each moment. Intuition is the voice, the expression, of this inner presence. If we listen to this voice, we receive guidance, direction and healing for the continued evolution of our soul.

Learning to listen to this silent inner voice requires only trust that it, indeed, exists. Most people, especially in the Western world, have been trained to place faith in only that which is experienced through the five physical senses and the rational mind. We are taught that if we cannot prove something through physical or scientific means, it is not true or valid. When opening and listening to intuition, we will not have that same type of proof. We must rely on inner guidance that may or may not coincide with outer, consensus, physical reality. I point this out so that you will not fall into the traps of doubt, distrust or fear in the process.

Also, be aware that although intuition is distinctly different from rational thoughts generated by the mind, it often intertwines with those thoughts when it comes through; in other words, the intuitive flow frequently shows up in the form of thought, even though it is not of mental origin. This interweaving helps in the delivery and interpretation of the information. For instance, I've told clients that loved ones on the other side use inspiration to get through to them. These thoughts may feel as if they are coming from the mind of the receiver when, in fact, they are not. In many readings, spirits impress their energy on my thoughts to convey their messages, which I then convey using language by way of my rational mind.

Of course, not all intuition is received through thought. Clairsentience is the experience of having a sensation or emotion that is not coming from the receiver. Likewise, dream visitations from the other side are frequently non-rational and seldom involve thinking.

In the beginning of my own development, I found that the more I used my intuitive and psychic abilities, the stronger they became. Over time, I was amazed at how clearly I could hear and follow my intuition, in addition to reading the energy of others. I quickly learned that everything in the physical world transmits energy, which can be detected by tuning into the inner senses. Further, I discovered that this energy is as real as electricity, for example, even though it cannot be seen physically. Just like gravity, intuition operates regardless of our conscious awareness of it. Energy is "honest" in the sense that it cannot be concealed, if we are trained to read it and trust our impressions.

In the course of your development, I recommend keeping a journal that is dedicated to your spiritual awareness. In most of the workshops I've taught, I encourage students to write about their experiences, immediately following the meditation exercises we've done in class. Writing helps to build intent and focus, two of the fundamental principles needed when opening intuitively. You may also discover that what you write comes from your soul through the vehicle of language. Don't try to analyze the words that come; allow them to flow.

I encourage you to develop intimacy with your Higher Self by applying daily the principles in this chapter. Above all, don't become discouraged if your initial expectations are not met. At first, you may receive insights that may be cloudy or undefined at best. The preferred course to follow is one that is patient and persistent. Relaxing into the process takes trust, time and practice. Before too long, you will recognize the distinct whisper of your inner voice.

The Higher Self Communicates Divine Wisdom

I have sat with hundreds of people who, for one reason or another, carry the weight of unresolved problems in their lives. As you have seen in the stories in Part Two, many seek to lift these burdens through making a connection to those in spirit and, hopefully, to Divine Spirit. No matter what the circumstance, people intuitively sense that they have reached the end of the road as far as dealing with life in an ego-centered way. In most readings, my spirit guides will impress me to guide people to find the spiritual essence within themselves, the Higher Self, in order to heal.

How does communicating with the Higher Self help to positively transform us? Aligning with this internal guidance system provides us with the incomparable advantage of navigating with much greater ease through life's challenges. It costs nothing, is continually available and is accessed conveniently by going within. Connecting with the Higher Self gives direct access to the sacred expression of the Divine as it manifests through us and our lives. This limitless resource knows exactly what we need and when. It is always aware of precisely where we are on the pathway of life.

The ego, by contrast, is a projection of our mind, as is the personality. Most people experience life through their minds, thoughts and emotions, which are all ego-based. Even people who consider themselves religious are often restricted by mental constructs and beliefs. Problems in life do not arise with having the thoughts themselves; after all, the mind is doing what it is designed to do: think. Rather, difficulties emerge when we *identify* with those thoughts and remain unaware that our core identity lies beyond those thoughts. Unfortunately, the resulting self-created dramas and traumas of life then take precedence over the spiritual reality of our being. If you have doubts about this being true, I encourage you to watch the daily news on television for five minutes and observe the chaos that human egos create.

An important point to remember is that the ultimate reward of developing spiritual consciousness is the creation of a more harmonious, heart-centered life. Don't buy into the mistaken belief that in order to do this, you must live on an isolated mountaintop somewhere meditating endlessly. Nor does it mean that you will eliminate your ego or personality. Rather, heightening awareness of your Higher Self requires living in the physical world and simultaneously knowing that you are Spirit. This necessitates accepting your own and others' egos exactly as they are, but not being a servant to those egos. I like to think of this as befriending the ego, taking it by the hand and inviting it along on the pathway of spiritual self-discovery. I've found this to be much easier than denying or resisting its influence.

There are several fundamental differences between the voice of the ego and the Higher Self. When you are in doubt, ask yourself these questions:

Does the voice inside feel "big" or "small?" To clarify, check inside to see how you feel physically about the guidance. Your body is a wonderful gauge to determine what is real and valid for you. Higher Self guidance will feel relaxing and tension-free. Your breathing will be natural, deep and centered in your solar plexus. In contrast, ego-based thoughts will feel more restrictive. Your breath will feel shallow, light and coming from the upper chest area.

Does the guidance given consider the good of all concerned? The Higher Self communicates from a universally loving perspective, a "we" versus "me" vantage point—the BP I first described in

Chapter Two. For example, if you ask for insight about forgiveness, Higher Self guidance would be positive and unconditionally loving in its tone. It will probably give you insight about the other person's point of view and the basis for their actions. The Higher Self seeks and exists in cooperation, harmony and unity. The ego will talk to you in terms of self-righteousness, self-protection and self-justification for holding onto resentments towards the other person. It seeks and exists in self-defense, chaos and separation, often at the expense of our highest good.

Does the guidance support your soul's true expression? In other words, when you receive inner guidance, does it feel as if it supports your soul's spiritual evolution or does it primarily concern a temporary, self-serving need? Following the divine direction of the Higher Self leads to freedom, not restriction, of being. Although it may often seem as if the ego's voice is justified, it is, by nature, limiting, since its frame of reference is centered on fortifying its own identity. Its voice satisfies immediate gratification and is short-sighted. Higher Self guidance is inclusive and far-sighted in its range.

Does the voice come from a place of love or fear? Your divine essence knows only love, wholeness and trust. By contrast, the ego frequently operates from a basis of fear since it perceives anything outside of itself as a threat to its own well being. It does not recognize the inherent good in all situations, despite the challenges involved. The Higher Self emanates from unwavering, unconditional compassion, while the ego comes from a place of uncertainty and distrust.

Becoming aware of how your ego operates greatly diminishes its ability to negatively influence you. Recognizing the difference between it and your "real" self gives you the ability to detach from the past, along with any self-defeating thoughts and emotional reactions to life.

If we open ourselves to receive it, the Higher Self perpetually shines through the hazy clouds of thoughts and emotions that ultimately cannot obscure its radiance. Its message is bright, clear: Wake up to the reality and magnitude of who you really are.

Who Am I?

A few years ago, Patty came to see me for a session in which she wanted to know what direction her family should take following her husband Ted's recent unexpected loss of a management position he had held for 33 years in a large corporation. From the moment I sat down with her, it was clear that Patty was extremely agitated and fearful about the sudden changes that had caused her formerly secure world to crash to the ground. She wanted to know what she should do. With Ted's job loss, everything she and her family had taken for granted for many years would deteriorate due to the loss of income. Moreover, Ted was so attached to his work that she feared he would sink into a depression over the job loss. She asked me if I felt the family would make it through this rough time.

"Yes," I answered. "But only if you wake up and realize that you and your family were never defined by Ted's job to begin with. If not, you will continue to feel insecure, uncertain and afraid. You must recognize that none of you, in reality, can be diminished by an outside event. Do you understand?"

Patty looked at me quizzically then said, "I just wanted to know if all of the investments we had made were going to get us through the lean times. What do you see about that?"

"Well, yes, but that's not the point I'm trying to communicate to you," I replied. "What I mean is, do you understand that you and your family are not defined or limited by Ted's job loss? Your true identity lies beyond anything that is in the outside world. It's understandable to be fearful when something like this happens, but don't let it control you because you are much, much larger than any job or even the fear of losing it. You need to realize that."

Patty was silent. I could tell by the expression on her face that this was not the guidance she had expected to hear. But I knew it was Spirit speaking through me to give her the reassurance she desperately needed to hear.

She let out a heavy sigh. "Well, okay. I'll remember what you said. I've been in a panic since Ted got the news. I guess now we all have to accept that things will be different, but somehow we'll get through this. Thanks for making me see the light."

As the above story illustrates, we will undoubtedly face unexpected, sometimes devastating, changes in life. How we adapt to those changes is directly dependent on the level of spiritual awareness we possess. If we believe ourselves to be victims of outside circumstances rather than observers of those events, we have become detached from the indomitable strength that comes from within. Realizing that conditions in the physical realm—jobs, relationships, money, health and death—are, by nature, transitory, helps to alleviate suffering when those conditions change. This is not to say that we do not or should not have feelings about change or loss. By all means, we should acknowledge those feelings and work through them. But our real power, which is found within, is always present beyond emotions and thoughts generated by our mind or outside events.

Consider this: Recall a recent time in which you had to cope with a tough challenge in life. How did you handle it? Did you give more of your energy (thoughts, attitudes and feelings) to the transitory outside world than to the permanent presence of Spirit anchored within? Walking through change and difficulties in life offers you the opportunity to become intimate with who you are beyond who you thought you were. Here is an important truth to remember: Illusions such as fear, anger and grief that you've allowed yourself to get lost in cannot exist in the light of your true self, nor can any experience that happens to you define or lessen who you really are. When you intuitively know this, you will be free and at peace.

The Inner Senses

In the first chapter, I mentioned that the inner senses of clairvoyance, clairaudience and clairsentience are the three main pathways through which I receive information. You do not have to be a medium to be aware of and use this form of silent communication to improve the quality of your life; anyone can do it with proper awareness and practice. Relying on these senses gives you the ability to decipher and follow your soul's pathway, as well as read the energy of the world around you.

Unlike the five physical senses, the inner senses are concerned with delivering and interpreting non-physical reality. Most people are naturally more developed in one sense than another, although that can change with time and practice. In spiritually developed individuals, all three senses weave a tapestry in the way they function. Years ago, my strongest inner sense was clairsentience. As I did more readings by phone, clairaudience opened and improved. Clairvoyance came years later. Today, all three senses are equally strong for me.

You are no doubt already using your inner senses without even being aware of it. Have you felt attracted to certain people and repelled by others for no logical reason? Have you had the experience of walking into a room, house or building that didn't feel right to you but you weren't sure why? Maybe you have experienced a gut-level knowing about a situation in your life without having any external evidence to prove it. In all of these cases and probably more, your inner senses were delivering information about the energy around you. You've been using the inners senses since the day you were born and now you are expanding this natural ability to perceive even more.

A note: In the beginning, it's best to allow the flow of your intuition to come in whatever way it reveals itself. As you will see, trusting your impressions, instead of doubting them, opens the gateway to intuition.

Becoming Spiritually FIT

There are three basic principles that can be applied to unlocking your intuition: focus, intent and trust. I call these the FIT trio because if you use them, you will become "spiritually fit." These principles will open and fortify your innate ability to hear the wisdom of Spirit within.

Focus gives you the laser-sharp lens you need to zero in on what you are sensing energy-wise and to discern the specific qualities of that energy, which I'll discuss later. The best way to increase focus is by practicing meditation for at least 15 minutes a day; or you can go into short periods of stillness several times a day. At the start of each meditation, use your breath as a focusing tool by placing your attention on it, allowing it to direct your awareness inward. Because the breath is always happening in the present moment, it shifts your mind's focus from the past or future.

Using a short prayer before each meditation will also help you to focus. This acts as a signal to your Higher Self to begin communicating what it is sensing.

Intent answers the questions "For what purpose am I doing this?" and "What do I want to discover in this particular intuitive exercise?" If you want to gain insight about some facet of your life, for example, I suggest writing that intention in your journal in the form of a question. Use clear, simple words and sentences to maintain focus. Then go into stillness. Immediately afterwards, write about the impressions and insights you received.

In cases where you are seeking insight for yourself, ask for the highest and best guidance about the situation to be revealed. I'm a firm believer in practical intuition, so I often set the intent for that type of information to come through. In other words, what steps can I take now to improve this situation? For instance, when I asked for insights about what I could specifically do concerning my health, the information that came through included practical changes in diet, rest, exercise and stress reduction. Intuition works hand-in-hand with the rational mind, so it's best to include it in the process.

The third principle of development- trust- is one that many people struggle with because of interference from their rational mind. Remember that, in most cases, you will not have immediate validation about the information you receive. (The exception to this is if you are reading the energy of another person who can immediately confirm your impressions.) Trust is the golden key that unlocks the door to your inner senses and the guidance of your soul. You must disregard the opinions that come from your rational mind long enough to feel the gentle flow of your intuition. Unfortunately, there is no short-cut that leads to trust. Just know that if you are having trouble in this area, you are not alone. Once again, time and patience are required in the process.

Balance Your Energy Before Tuning In

In-depth spiritual work requires preparation. Just as we plan and perform preliminary measures prior to undertaking any important task in life, we must prepare to journey within by first becoming ready to do so. Before engaging in any intuitive work, it's necessary for you to first ground and harmonize your vital life-force energy. This is important to do because if you are stressed, emotionally unbalanced or ill, you may not receive clear or accurate impressions. In the case of illness, it's often advisable to wait until you are feeling better. I know from personal experience that being emotionally unbalanced leads to less than optimal results. I make every effort to eliminate or detach from personal "drama" that may affect the quality of my work.

The following exercises are simple and safe to do in your intuitive practice. Combined, they will take about eight to 10 minutes. Becoming aware of and managing your own energy field will help you to maintain balance, focus and clarity.

Ground yourself in several ways: First focus on your breath, allowing it to pull you inside to stillness. Next, focus on the energy center at the base of your spine, the root. This center energetically anchors your spiritual essence with your physical body. Think of the roots of a tree or plant which draw nutrients from the earth. As you place your attention on this center, imagine that a thick cord emanates from it into the earth. Now feel the connection between this center, your legs, feet and the earth. Breathe deeply. Imagine that you are anchored securely to the earth by this cord. Feel the contact between your feet and the surface they rest upon for a few moments.

Another way to ground is by lying on the floor. Start with breath awareness. Then feel the contact of your body with the earth by becoming aware of the floor beneath you. Focus on the lower back area and feet. "Breathe into" these areas of your body for a few minutes.

The third grounding technique is to go outside and sit or lie on the ground, or sit with your back against a tree. After following your breath for a few minutes, focus on your tailbone. See the thick cord (mentioned in the first exercise) going deeply into the ground beneath you. Breathe deeply and relax.

Now, shift your attention to the energy center at the top of your head, the crown. Through this center, the divine life essence connects with your body. Next, imagine a brilliant white or violet light flowing down from the cosmos into the top of your head. See that light travel down your spinal column through the root center and out the bottom of both feet. Now see it circulate back to the top of your head and flow down again. Do this several times as you breathe deeply.

To harmonize your energy field, focus your attention on the

center of your chest, near your physical heart. Breathe into this center. Then think of a person or animal you love very much. It doesn't matter if these souls are living or deceased. See their faces, look into their eyes and open your heart to send love. If you want, see the love you send as pink light that emanates from your heart to theirs. Feel your heart infused with love from those you have sent love to. Breathe deeply. Now slowly return by focusing on your breath. Open your eyes and move your hands and feet. You are now ready to begin your intuitive work.

A Meditation to Meet Your Higher Self

In your journal, write a question you want to obtain insight about. This could be about any situation, circumstance or relationship in your life. Be as specific as you can and make the question about yourself (not others.) You will return to your journal later after the meditation. Even though I've used the generic masculine pronoun in reference to the Higher Self, this can appear to you as female, an animal, or you may experience it as light or color. As always, it's preferable to be open when entering into this meditation.

After doing the preliminary grounding and centering exercise, focus on your breath. After a few moments, see in your mind's eye a radiant column of white light in front of you. This light is brilliantly pulsating in its purity. It is safe for you to step into this column of white light to travel to meet with your Higher Self.

As you merge with the column of white light, feel yourself drifting higher and higher. You are becoming lighter and freer. That sense of freedom becomes stronger and stronger as you travel. Feel yourself gently touch down in a beautiful place in nature, a radiant summer garden, a beautiful meadow or a quiet forest. In this special place, you will meet with your Higher Self.

Use all of your inner senses to feel this inner guide. Sense the energy. Feel its presence and embrace. Pay attention to any sensations in your physical body that you experience in the presence of the Higher Self; for example, you may feel tingling or warmth, or you may feel expanded beyond your body. Whatever you feel, simply note this and remember it.

Your Higher Self now brings you a message about the question you wrote in your journal. The message appears in a way that you easily recognize and understand. It may be in symbolic form or you may be shown an image that gives you insight. How does it feel to you emotionally? How does it feel intuitively? Does it bring comfort? Is further investigation needed?

Make note of any words or phrases that come from your Higher Self. Are there feelings that accompany these? Is there an image that appears on your inner viewing screen?

If the Higher Self appears to you as a person, pay attention to the way he is dressed and his demeanor. Are there any distinguishing characteristics? Ask your Higher Self to be with you each day, giving you guidance and inspiration. Realize that you and this guide are one. There is no separation.

As you return to normal waking state through the white column of light, feel your hands, feet and body. Open your eyes and take a deep breath. In your journal, write about the impressions you received during the meditation.

Note: A recorded version of this meditation is on my 3 CD set, *Igniting Your Spiritual Intuition.*

Determining Qualities of Energy

When I first started doing readings, the information I received was "blurry" and non-specific. Over time and with much practice and training, my abilities have refined considerably. For me, that development has made all the difference in the world as far as giving more direct, specific messages to help people. But you don't have to be a medium to increase your innate ability to read energy; you can still benefit from sharpening your intuitive skills. All you need are moderate doses of determination, patience and trust in the process.

Determining the quality of energetic impressions refers to the ability to discern differences in their speed, vibration, color, sound and texture. As I stated earlier, focus is the lens through which you will gain clarity about what you perceive. It is also needed to help you discern specific qualities of whatever you tune into. Therefore, improving focus helps you to fine-tune your inner senses to discern what you perceive. The following guidelines will help you do this:

Before meditation, set the intention to receive specific impressions about what you are focusing on. During meditation, ask for the clearest impressions possible to come to you. Ask Spirit to show you specific qualities of what you are observing. Ask for crystal clarity in sensing everything you will need to perceive at the time.

Zero in on what you perceive through clairvoyance. Imagine that your internal viewing screen is a large-screen TV, on which you can see the finest details. Then imagine pushing a zoom lens on the TV that allows you to capture the specifics of what you are viewing.

Pay attention to how impressions of different energies make you feel physically. As stated earlier, the physical body is a good indicator of what is going on an intuitive, energetic level. For example, imagine that you perceive a symbol or energetic impression in meditation. Is there a physical sensation that accompanies the symbol? What part of your body do you feel this in? Check in to see if your body feels relaxed or tense, comfortable or queasy and warm or cold.

With clairvoyance, imagine you are holding the object you perceive in your hand. What does it feel like? Is it soft, hard or neutral? Is it hollow or solid? Light or heavy? Zoom back in your mind's eye and observe it from all angles. What does this reveal? Note the color, size, texture and weight of the object.

To hear Spirit speak more clearly, turn up your internal speakers to listen. It may sound silly but to hear Spirit more clearly, imagine there is a set of internal speakers in your brain. Before meditation, imagine turning the volume up on the control panel for the speaker system. Then tune into what is received through these speakers during meditation.

I suggest that you keep track of impressions you get during meditation by writing them in your journal. You can then review your own spiritual "messages" anytime you desire.

Connecting with the Spirit World

When I teach people how to connect with the other side, I explain that the ability to receive this type of communication comes about by tuning into the "broadcast" of the spirit world, which is perceived through the inner senses of the receiver. Developing this type of sensitivity is much like honing intuition in that it requires time, trust and patience. Not everyone is destined to become a medium but many people want to feel, hear and see their own loved ones who have passed into spirit. Learning to communicate with the spirit world is much like learning a new language, one that is non-verbal, intuitive and inspirational. Although most languages follow rules of grammar—much like "i" before "e" in the English language—communication with the other side does not because it comes through the non-linear, right-hemisphere of the brain. Impressions received in this way will come through symbols, feelings, sensations of energy and synchronicities.

If you're sincerely drawn to give messages to others, it's best to start your training by taking basic intuition development classes to open and expand your inner senses. I recommend taking a series of classes or intensive workshops with reputable, experienced mediums who will support, mentor and guide you along the way. When you are comfortable with trusting your inner senses, you will naturally begin to sense spirits and communication from the other side. Don't be discouraged if this doesn't happen at first. To help you in your development, meet regularly and often with others who are on the same spiritual pathway and exchange impressions. This will give you validation, encouragement and perseverance on your journey.

If you aren't interested in taking classes but still want to heighten your ability to sense loved ones in spirit, try this: Before meditating, place a photo of your loved one(s) nearby. Begin by focusing on your breath. Ask your loved one to be with you by giving you some sort of sign or validation, preferably something that is easily recognizable. This could be anything: a light touch on your head or shoulders, a tingling sensation on your arms, a feeling of well being or an image you see through clairvoyance. This sign will be your loved one's calling card or identification. Each time this sign appears in the future, you will recognize your loved one.

After identification is established, ask your spirit loved ones to communicate to you in other ways. In *I'm Still with You*, I wrote about signs of after-death communication, or ADC's, from the other side that people receive without the assistance of a medium. These remarkable occurrences frequently come in the form of physical phenomena but can also appear through dreams, energetic sensations and inspiration. I believe spirits create these to give reassurance and comfort to surviving family members after their deaths.

Perhaps you've been fortunate enough to receive one of these gifts from the other side and it has provided confirmation that death isn't the end of the soul. If you haven't, don't be disappointed. In the course of grieving, the worst thing you can do is hold onto rigid expectations about when or how loved ones will communicate. It's the easiest way to become discouraged, which will dampen your ability to perceive communication when it does happen. Instead, ask loved ones to visit you in dreams or by inspiring you in everyday life. Then be open to receive this form of communication.

You and deceased loved ones already possess the strongest characteristic necessary to communicate with one another: love. In all the readings I've done, it is the single unifying, all-encompassing factor that endures, despite the illusion of separation between souls. Sending positive thoughts and prayer to those in spirit strengthens the bond you share with them and helps both of you to heal.

Keep in mind that loved ones impress us with their thoughts without our conscious awareness. For instance, have you thought of someone who has passed into spirit while you were daydreaming, doing a simple task or relaxing? It is often the case that that person is sending thoughts to you, even though it doesn't register with you in that way. Here's a recent example from my life:

Not long ago, I visited Lilydale, New York, the largest American center for the religion of Spiritualism, where I've taught and taken classes on mediumship. As I walked past the quaint rows of Victorian houses adorned with hanging baskets overflowing with colorful flowers, I encountered Lynn, a resident medium who was tending to her garden. As we chatted briefly, I spotted several bright, magenta-colored snap-dragons in Lynn's garden, which instantly sparked a memory from my early childhood about my mother, who had also grown snap-dragons. Thinking back to that day, I remembered that I thought it was amusing to trap a bee within the flower by closing the lip of the flower around the insect. My mother, who was standing nearby, rushed over and pulled me away from the flower, warning me that I could get stung. As I reflected on this childhood memory, it occurred to me that less than 15 minutes earlier, I had made another reference about my mother (who had passed eight years earlier) to another acquaintance I had seen on my walk around Lilydale. I didn't often talk about memories of my mom, especially to mere acquaintances. Now, talking with Lynn, I felt my mom's comforting presence around me. The impression was soft, reassuringly familiar and soothing, just as Mom had been in life.

Did Mom really come to me in a spiritual sense? I believe so. It certainly made sense that she would choose to come through in Lilydale, which has been a center for spirit communication for more than a century. It was her way of letting me know she was still with me.

Reconnection with those we have loved in life is facilitated by feeling appreciation and gratitude for the relationship we shared with them, even if the relationship was challenging. Healing grief and coming to terms with difficult relationships requires a review of what relationships have taught us spiritually, soul to soul. Getting in touch with this level of awareness frees us to love ourselves and others unconditionally.

Expectations Suppress Spiritual Awareness

You've no doubt heard the old expression that curiosity killed the cat. When it comes to working with Spirit, rigid, inflexible attitudes and expectations kill spiritual awareness. Some people have an attitude of what I call "prove it to me" in regard to mediumship and other spiritual activities. I have often explained that this type of communication is not black and white, like reading a book or newspaper. Feelings, impressions and intuition don't always make sense to the logical brain, yet are nonetheless valid and just as real as verbal communication.

If you are considering whether or not to have a reading and you are looking for proof of life beyond death or the reality of spirit communication beyond a shadow of a doubt, I encourage you to not have it until you have released your expectations about what will be communicated. On the other hand, you should not be so accepting that you try to make messages fit when they clearly do not apply. If your attitude about the subject falls somewhere in between these two extremes, you will probably be pleasantly surprised at what comes through during a reading. A good rule of thumb is that a session should confirm loved ones' identity and presence around you, which, in turn, provides reassurance, healing and peace.

I'll address expectations by using this analogy: Have you ever had the experience of someone telling you about how fabulous a movie was and then being disappointed when you saw the same movie because it fell short of your expectations? That is what happens when people come for sessions or do spiritual work with preconceived notions or personal agendas. The other side cannot effectively communicate through our pre-set beliefs. So how do you avoid this pitfall? In the case of readings, it's best to come prepared with questions you'd like insight on but be open to other information that is communicated. The other side comes through with helpful insights regarding these questions but also has its own perspective (the BP) about what should be communicated. Maintaining a receptive attitude allows the reading to flow smoothly.

Insisting that the communication be delivered in the way you want is the quickest way to deflate a session. I've delivered what I consider excellent readings in which clients' family members communicate substantial validating evidence only to hear clients complain afterwards about why another relative didn't come through. I've also given readings in which people "hold out" for an unreasonably high level of proof from the other side before becoming receptive to the communication. In both cases, clients' expectations seriously dilute the impact of the session. I'm not suggesting that you make information fit when clearly it doesn't; instead be open to whom and what is communicated. In many instances, some information given during readings cannot or will not be validated until later.

Willingness, honesty, trust and open-mindedness are central to taking charge of your life by doing spiritually focused self-improvement work. Demanding that things be done our way or in our time restricts the natural flow of Spirit. I encourage you to always ask for the highest and best good to come to you from the abundance that the universe has to offer. Then let go of the need to control the outcome.

Daily Maintenance of the Spiritual Senses

Just as physical exercise helps to sustain a healthy body, using the inner senses regularly strengthens and improves them. The surest way to keep the spiritual senses open and vital is through daily meditation and prayer. The following are guidelines to help you maintain spiritual health:

Keep your mediations short and focused (no longer than 15 or 20 minutes.) You are less inclined to drift. Write a question in your journal and ask for insight during meditation. Record the experiences, insights and wisdom you obtain. This also applies to dreams in which your Higher Self communicates to you.

Designate a space in your home in which to meditate. Place objects that are sacred to you in that space. Meditate in this space around the same time every day. Your rational brain will learn to anticipate and adapt to the quiet time. It will then be easier for you to turn off your thoughts.

Do not become discouraged if you find yourself thinking during meditation. It is normal and natural for the rational brain to churn out thoughts during still time. When this happens, refocus your attention on your breath. Do this as many times as is necessary.

If you listen to music during meditation, vary it. You want to stay alert, not bored, during the time you spend with Spirit. Remember that you can meditate anywhere, anytime, except when driving or when your full attention is required.

When you pray, picture the desired outcome as if it is reality, then let go and trust the situation is healed. Always ask for the best for yourself and others, remembering that you may not know exactly what that is. If you are praying for a person's health, for example, see her as healthy and happy. Ask for divine will, not yours, to be realized during prayer. It is impossible to determine the outcome for others because of their free will. Release the results of prayer to Spirit.

Practice developing your intuition by purchasing a set of cards designed for that purpose. The tarot, although complex, is an excellent divination tool for spiritual insight. You will need to buy a book about the meaning of the tarot or take a class to learn the meanings of the 78 cards. Any of the angel decks (which are much simpler to understand) by Doreen Virtue are also helpful. Pull one card or several cards daily and tune into how it applies to your life. Offer to do this for family or friends to gain experience.

Rune casting is an ancient system of divination first used in the Norse culture. The runes (typically made from stone or wood) symbolize the power found in the four elements of nature. The various runes that come up after casting will give insight and direction to your focus and questions.

Gratitude for blessings in your life reinforces awareness of Spirit in self and others. Look around and appreciate how this wondrous, divine presence manifests in your life and the world. Acknowledge the Divine within by giving thanks daily.

The Pathway at the End of the Road

On a busy road near my home, there is a large magnetic sign belonging to a chiropractic office that displays inspirational wisdom. A few weeks ago, the sign read: *At the end of the road, there is a pathway.* Each time I passed the sign, I considered what this simple sentence might imply. Several interpretations came to mind: Could the "end of the road" mean the end of suffering in life and the "pathway" represent our rising above it? Is the pathway symbolic of the higher life in spirit we embrace after ending our journey here on earth? If the road represents life, then the pathway at the end represents the continuation of our soul in spirit after we exit the thoroughfare of physical existence.

Another possible meaning came to mind: A pathway is typically narrower than a road, thus implying that we must follow the voice of our own soul and not that of the masses. Meeting the challenge of finding that inner voice may lead us down roads that are less traveled by others, as Robert Frost eloquently expressed in his famous poem, *The Road Not Taken*. At times, stepping onto the pathway requires all the courage we can muster to conquer the looming fear that threatens to overtake us. The journey that stretches before us may appear strange, lonely and uncertain. Yet is there any other way to go besides being true to who we really are?

In the quest to know ourselves more deeply, we are presented with a wealth of opportunities to discover and explore the brilliancy of Spirit that is present in each moment. As the stories in these chapters illustrate, relationships offer us mirrors that reflect the Divine to us again and again. While navigating the peaks and valleys of life, if we keep the primary relationship we have with Spirit intact, our human relationships will assuredly reflect that love. In truth, all pathways, no matter what their origin, lead to the destination of awakening to the Divine within.

* * *

You and I are living in a world today in which fear is increasingly being brought into humankind's conscious awareness so that it can be clearly recognized and cleansed in the light of a higher spiritual consciousness. We stand at a crossroads, faced with far-reaching choices which have the power to either make or break us as a species. In the midst of this chaos of change, the only question that is really relevant is whether we are willing to survive and prosper through working together in harmony or destroy ourselves through ignorance and separation.

As you read these words, know that you are part of a significant shift taking place in the evolution of human beings and the planet. As our old, ego-centered consciousness crumbles, we are moving towards greater unity and compassion. Your physical presence on the earth is not an accident; it is your soul's plan to evolve through all of your life's experiences. You are here at this time to express Spirit through your personality, talents and service, which no one but you can manifest. Through the example of your contributions, others who struggle will be encouraged and inspired to follow their unique pathway. Know that your life affects many others, even though you may not be aware of it. Your conscious choice to live in love, peace and with compassion will attract others who will join you on your pathway.

Take heart that you are never alone during times of difficulty. The angels, spirit guides and spirit loved ones watch over you. As your spiritual awareness increases, you will feel their loving presence and guidance support you when the going gets tough. No matter what obstacle you encounter, do not let it deter you from living with faith, hope and optimism.

No matter what the past has brought you, it holds no power over you now. Know this and be free! If it has been painful, use your experiences of healing to comfort and uplift others who suffer. Be the light! At all times, align yourself with truth and love the world. Take solace in this comforting message from Spirit: You, as an eternal soul, are forever connected with every other soul who has gone before you through love. In this truth, be at peace.

Recommended Resources

Buckland's Book of Spirit Communications by Raymond Buckland. Woodbury, MN: Llewllyn Worldwide, Ltd, 2004.

A Course in Miracles by the Foundation for Inner Peace. Glen Ellen, CA: the Foundation for Inner Peace, 1976. www.acim.org.

A Journey Into Light (meditation CD) by Robin Miller. Millsong Music Publishing (ASCAP), Robin Miller Productions, 2005.

A New Earth: Finding Your Life's Purpose by Eckhart Tolle. New York: Penguin Group, 2005. www.eckherttolletv.com. (for live podcasts, online talks and courses.)

The Silent Path (meditation CD) by Robert Haig Coxon. Quebec, Canada: R.H.C. Productions, 1995.

12step.org (website). Resources and information about the 12 step program.

Your Soul's Plan: Discovering the Real Meaning of the Life You Planned Before You Were Born by Robert Schwartz. Berkeley: Frog Books, 2009.

Carole J. Obley (Soulvisions, LLC) is an acclaimed spiritual medium and author who has delivered thousands of evidentiary messages from the spirit world to people seeking confirmation of life after death and healing from grief. Her work has been featured in newspaper articles and she speaks regularly in the media. In addition to maintaining a private practice in mediumship near Pittsburgh, Pa., she presents seminars and workshops on mediumship and spiritual development. She may be contacted through her website, **www.soulvisions.net**

6th Books investigates the paranormal, supernatural, explainable or unexplainable. Titles cover everything included within parapsychology: how to, lifestyles, beliefs, myths, theories and memoir.